Cambridge Elements ≡

Elements in European Politics
edited by
Catherine De Vries
Bocconi University
Gary Marks
University of North Carolina at Chapel Hill and European University Institute

POLITICAL CHANGE AND ELECTORAL COALITIONS IN WESTERN DEMOCRACIES

Peter A. Hall
Harvard University

Georgina Evans
Harvard University

Sung In Kim
Harvard University

CAMBRIDGE
UNIVERSITY PRESS

Shaftesbury Road, Cambridge CB2 8EA, United Kingdom

One Liberty Plaza, 20th Floor, New York, NY 10006, USA

477 Williamstown Road, Port Melbourne, VIC 3207, Australia

314–321, 3rd Floor, Plot 3, Splendor Forum, Jasola District Centre, New Delhi – 110025, India

103 Penang Road, #05–06/07, Visioncrest Commercial, Singapore 238467

Cambridge University Press is part of Cambridge University Press & Assessment, a department of the University of Cambridge.

We share the University's mission to contribute to society through the pursuit of education, learning and research at the highest international levels of excellence.

www.cambridge.org
Information on this title: www.cambridge.org/9781009431347

DOI: 10.1017/9781009431378

First published 2023

A catalogue record for this publication is available from the British Library.

ISBN 978-1-009-43134-7 Paperback
ISSN 2754-5032 (online)
ISSN 2754-5024 (print)

Political Change and Electoral Coalitions in Western Democracies

Elements in European Politics

DOI: 10.1017/9781009431378
First published online: June 2023

Peter A. Hall
Harvard University

Georgina Evans
Harvard University

Sung In Kim
Harvard University

Author for correspondence: Peter A. Hall, phall@fas.harvard.edu

Abstract: This Element documents long-term changes in the political attitudes of occupational groups, shifts in the salience of economic and cultural issues, and the movement of political parties in the electoral space from 1990 to 2018 in eight Western democracies. We evaluate prominent contentions about how electoral contestation has changed and why support for mainstream parties has declined while support for challenger parties has increased. We contribute a new analysis of how the viability of the types of electoral coalitions assembled by center-left, center-right, radical-right, and Green parties changes over these decades. We find that their viability is affected by changes over time in citizens' attitudes to economic and cultural issues and shifts in the relative salience of those issues. We examine the contribution these developments make to declining support for mainstream center-left and center-right coalitions and increasing support for coalitions underpinning radical-right and Green parties.

Keywords: electoral coalitions, issue salience, party competition, populism

ISBNs: 9781009431347 (PB), 9781009431378 (OC)
ISSNs: 2754-5032 (online), 2754-5024 (print)

Contents

1 Introduction

The past thirty years have seen dramatic changes in the electoral politics of Western democracies. Among the most important is a substantial decline in the share of votes secured by mainstream parties of the center-left and center-right. Its mirror image has been rising electoral support for challengers, including Green parties and parties on the radical-right and radical-left (see Figure 1). A familiar postwar politics built on cleavages of social class and religion has given way to something new and consequential for the types of policies governments are likely to be able to pursue (Evans 1999; Knutsen 2006; Mudde 2007; Kriesi et al. 2008; Hobolt and De Vries 2020).

Scholars are still grappling with questions about whether these developments represent dealignment or realignment around new cleavages and what they imply for the long-term fortunes of mainstream parties (Häusermann and Kriesi 2015; Hooghe and Marks 2018; Abou-Chadi and Wagner 2019; Gidron and Ziblatt 2019; Marks et al. 2021). However, the answers to such questions about the future turn on important questions about the past, namely: In what ways has the electoral landscape changed and what renders the electoral situation of mainstream parties more precarious? An impressive body of scholarship addresses those questions, albeit with competing contentions, and our objective is not to add to them. But most of the evidence adduced for these explanations is cross-sectional or based on data for relatively short periods of time. We lack clear portraits of how the positions of social groups within the electoral space have changed over the past thirty years and corresponding accounts of how the potential for various types of electoral coalitions has shifted in that period.[1]

Our objectives are to fill this gap and use the resulting evidence to consider how the viability of different types of electoral coalitions has shifted over this period with a view to assessing competing explanations for the decline of mainstream parties and the rise of their challengers. For these purposes, we examine the movements of people in seven occupational groups across a two-dimensional electoral space in eight Western democracies over the three decades from 1990 to 2018. Based on shifts in the attitudes of these groups to economic and cultural issues and the salience of those issues, we calculate the relative viability of four types of electoral coalitions corresponding to those often assembled by mainstream and challenger parties. We find evidence for many, but not all, explanations for the shifting electoral fortunes of these parties and for the contention that electoral competition now takes place along a new

---

[1] For parallel studies with different analytical ambitions, see Caughey et al. 2019, Gethin et al. 2022, and Kitschelt and Rehm 2022.

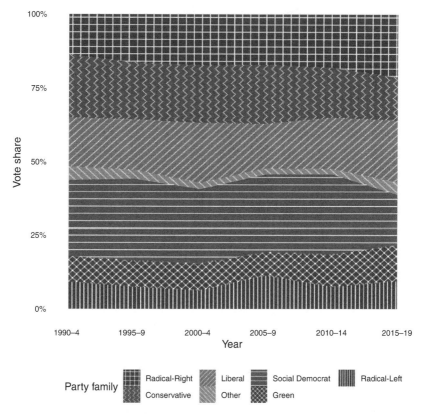

Figure 1 Share of votes for major party families in parliamentary elections 1990–2019.

Source: Data from Gethin et al. (2022) for the eight countries in this study smoothed over five years.

axis running from Green parties to radical-right parties which some scholars have associated with the rise of a new "transnational" cleavage.

1.1 Contemporary Contentions about Electoral Change

The contemporary literature contains a variety of propositions about how the shape of the electoral space has changed over the past thirty years and why support for mainstream parties has been declining. Some works advance several of these propositions, while others emphasize only one or two of them, but broadly speaking these contentions fall into three groups.

The first group emphasize the impact of secular economic and social changes on the attitudes and related policy preferences of voters. These developments can be said to affect the "demand side" of electoral politics. At their center is the decline of employment in the manufacturing sector, which once offered decent jobs to many blue-collar workers, and a corresponding increase in employment in services (Iversen and Cusack 2000). That long-term development gathered pace with globalization during the 1980s and 1990s, as many firms moved manufacturing jobs offshore to emerging economies (Baily and Lawrence 2004). At the same time, growing demand for services from both companies and consumers created many new jobs of various kinds in services. Oesch (2013a) calculates that the share of professionals and managers in the occupational structure of many advanced capitalist economies has increased by about 20 percent since the early 1990s. A new technological revolution in information technology is also shifting the occupational structure. By increasing the demand for highly skilled workers at the expense of those with medium levels of skill, it has eliminated many types of positions and polarized the occupational structures of some countries (Goos et al. 2009; Autor and Dorn 2013).

Over the same period of time, shifting social attitudes have created the potential for more intense conflict over cultural issues. This development also has long-term roots going back to the postmaterialist revolt of the late 1960s, which saw younger generations rebel against the materialist outlooks of their parents, embrace a more diverse set of lifestyles, and attach increasing importance to issues of social equality (Inglehart 1977). Those concerns found expression in the new social movements of the 1980s focused on nuclear disarmament, racial or gender equality, and environmental issues, which ultimately gave rise to Green parties and further social movements during the 1990s and 2000s, such as those seeking gay rights and access to abortion (Dalton and Kuechler 1990; Kriesi et al. 1995).

Four propositions about how the contemporary electoral space has changed are grounded in these observations.

H1. The most prominent of these is that economic developments associated with the decline of manufacturing, the growth of service-sector employment, and the transition to a knowledge economy have fragmented the occupational structure, thereby eroding the cleavage between a blue-collar working class and a white-collar middle class that was once central to European politics (Oesch 2008a; Beramendi et al. 2015; Iversen and Soskice 2015; Oesch and Rennwald 2018). That cleavage is said to have given way to a wider array of occupational groups with more heterogenous political preferences than those once held by blue- or white-collar workers, rooted in differences in occupational tasks, employment security, education, and income (Kitschelt and Rehm 2014; Gethin et al. 2022).

H2. Based on the cultural changes of recent years, most analyses of the electoral space also claim that, alongside the economic issues once central to electoral competition, a new set of cultural issues have become increasingly important to voters and salient to electoral competition. These are issues associated with gender equality, gay rights, abortion, and immigration.[2] As a result, new gaps on cultural issues have appeared between citizens, scattering them more widely across an electoral space that is now two-dimensional (Inglehart 1990; Kitschelt 1994; Kriesi et al. 2006; De Vries et al. 2013; Häusermann and Kriesi 2015).

H3. Among these accounts about the prevalence of cultural conflict, some stress the particular importance of a growing gap on cultural issues between blue-collar and white-collar workers, often ascribed to the reaction of blue-collar workers against the extent to which more educated employees have embraced cosmopolitan (or postmaterial/universalist) values (Norris and Inglehart 2019).

H4. Others postulate a new divergence in economic preferences between various segments of the working class, generally based on variations in employment security, although scholars disagree about the primary basis for this divergence. Some locate the division between secure labor market "insiders" and more precarious "outsiders" (Rueda 2005), some between workers with high levels of specific skills and low-skilled workers (Iversen and Soskice 2015), while others find a division between people in occupations facing higher versus lower levels of labor market risk (Häusermann et al. 2015; Schwander 2020).

A second set of propositions prominent in the literature about electoral change focuses on the contribution that the strategies of political parties have made to declining support for mainstream parties and rising support for their populist competitors. We can think of these as arguments about developments on the "supply side" of electoral politics.

H5. Some efforts to explain rising support for populist right parties attribute it to a reaction against the extent to which mainstream party platforms converged on neoliberal approaches to economic problems during the 1990s. These works cite two causal paths. One argument is that party platforms failed to represent the views of working-class voters on such issues, thereby inspiring political alienation and a protest vote for anti-establishment parties (Spruyt et al. 2016; Berger 2017; Berman and

---

[2] Although some analysts treat attitudes to immigration as a separate factor (Caughey et al. 2019; Lancaster 2022), and there are some grounds for doing so, in our factor analysis attitudes to immigration load in a congruent way with the other views we associate with cultural attitudes, and we treat it as a component of those attitudes in the interest of identifying a two-dimensional issue space (see Appendix C).

Snegovaya 2019; Hopkin and Blyth 2019; Hopkin 2020; Grant and Tilley 2022). Others argue that the convergence in party platforms on economic issues leads parties, seeking a distinctive basis for their appeals, to put more emphasis on cultural issues and that voters, seeking distinctive grounds on which to choose among parties, do so as well (Spies 2013; Ward et al. 2015). Since the attractiveness of most populist right parties turns heavily on their stance toward cultural issues, these dynamics should have worked to their advantage.

H6. A related but alternative argument suggests that rising support for populist right parties, especially among working-class voters, has been driven by the extent to which center-left parties, which were once their natural political home, have moved to embrace cosmopolitan (or postmaterialist) cultural values, often with a view to securing more votes from the middle class (Evans and Tilley 2017; Häusermann 2018; Gethin et al. 2022). The premises here are that many working-class voters hold more traditional values, were discouraged from voting for center-left parties by this move, and hence have become a promising reservoir of support for populist right parties that promote traditional values.

Finally, a third set of propositions prominent in the contemporary literature focuses on changes in the overall terms of electoral competition in the wake of these developments, and their consequences for the fate of mainstream and challenger parties.

H7. Some analysts posit that cultural issues have become much more salient to electoral competition in recent years relative to economic concerns, and ascribe rising support for right populist parties to the increasing salience of those issues, on the grounds that these parties appeal to voters primarily on cultural issues, such as the cultural threats putatively posed by immigrants, while mainstream parties are in decline because they rely more heavily for support on economic appeals, such as policies of income redistribution (Ivarsflaten 2005; Bornschier 2010; Häusermann and Kriesi 2015; Oesch and Rennwald 2018; Magistro and Wittstock 2021; Danieli et al. 2022).

H8. Putting these developments together, some scholars also argue that, in the wake of eroding class and religious alignments, electoral competition now turns on a new transnational (or universalist–particularist) cleavage that pits parties promoting cosmopolitan values and left-wing economic positions, including Green parties and some center-left parties, against populist right parties defending traditional values and more conservative economic positions. One implication is that the principal axis of political competition no longer runs horizontally along a standard left–right axis reflecting economic issues, but along a diagonal cutting across the new two-dimensional political space. Another implication is that Green parties and radical-right parties have become more important contenders for power, increasingly crucial to governing coalitions of the political left or right (Kriesi et al. 2006, 2008; Bornschier 2010; Häusermann and Kriesi 2015; Hooghe and Marks 2018; Rovny and Polk 2019a; Marks et al. 2021).

These are important contentions that, in one version or another, go some distance toward explaining why mainstream center-left and center-right parties have found it difficult to hold together the electoral coalitions that once kept them in office and why support for Green parties and parties of the populist right or left has increased. As such, they deserve careful scrutiny.

Of course, there are multiple ways in which some of these propositions can be tested, and we do not attempt anything like complete assessments here. But these contentions embody claims about: (1) how voters have moved in the electoral space over the past three decades; (2) how the salience of different types of issues has changed; (3) how party positions have shifted; and, ultimately, (4) how the viability of the electoral coalitions formed by different types of political parties has changed over these years. Those are the empirical issues addressed in this Element and, by examining them, we bring some evidence to bear on the plausibility of these eight contentions.

1.2 The Approach

Our first objective is to assess how the political attitudes of voters concerning economic and cultural issues, on which many political parties base their appeals, have changed over the past thirty years; and our second objective is to assess how the viability of the electoral coalitions that these parties might form from various groups of voters has shifted over recent decades. For these purposes, we consider groups of voters classified according to their position within the occupational structure and examine the movement of those groups within a two-dimensional issue space encompassing the positions taken by their members on economic and cultural issues. This approach to understanding how the viability of electoral coalitions changes has both limitations and advantages.

In our view, there is value in thinking in terms of electoral coalitions. The electoral success of political parties ultimately turns on how many votes they can secure and, except for the smallest of parties, securing those votes generally entails appealing to groups of people with diverse views. Accordingly, we focus on the process of coalition formation within the electorate. Our conception of how electoral coalitions are formed may be more controversial, because there are several different grounds on which people might vote for a party and hence different ways in which parties can form coalitions. Partisan appeals can be based on a party's reputation for competent governance or on its stance toward a valence issue such as corruption (Green and Jennings 2017; Hobolt and De Vries 2020). Alternatively, parties can appeal to the social identities of voters or attract them by disbursing goods in clientelist fashion (Kitschelt and Wilkinson 2007; Bornschier et al. 2021; Mierke-Zatwarnicki 2022). Coalition formation is inevitably a multifaceted process.

We focus, however, on the appeals that parties make to the political attitudes of voters, understood as the positions those voters take on a range of economic and cultural issues germane to electoral competition. Although appeals to political attitudes may not be the only basis for partisan support, it is difficult to imagine parties forming viable electoral coalitions without speaking to the political preferences of the voters who compose those coalitions (Goren 2013). In corresponding terms, we assess the viability of a given electoral coalition by reference to how well it aggregates the preferences of the groups of which it is composed. The results are inevitably somewhat stylized for the reasons we have noted, but we think that this is as likely as any other approach to capture the viability of alternative coalitions.

Parallel issues arise with respect to how the groups that make up electoral coalitions should be construed. In principle, these groups could be understood in any number of ways, including in terms of religion, ethnicity, gender, age, or region of residence. For effective cross-national comparison, however, we need a schema delineating groups whose members tend to have similar political preferences and preferences that vary in parallel ways across multiple countries. For these reasons, it makes sense to group voters based on their occupational class. Across countries, occupational class is systematically related to political preferences over the types of broad economic and cultural issues on which we concentrate (Kitschelt and Rehm 2014; Häusermann and Kriesi 2015; Oesch and Rennwald 2018; Marks et al. 2022). Occupation is also frequently used to delineate the groups forming electoral coalitions: hence, using this schema speaks to an important literature on class politics (Rydgren 2013; Beramendi et al. 2015). Accordingly, we chart the movement of occupational groups within a two-dimensional electoral space, reflecting the positions of those groups on economic and cultural issues, at three points in time over the period from 1990 to 2018. We then use this analysis to assess how and why the viability of alternative electoral coalitions changes over these decades.

2 The Movement of Citizens in the Electoral Space

For the purposes of this analysis, we need cross-national data from which comparable measures of citizens' attitudes concerning economic and cultural issues can be constructed, spanning the longest possible time period. The most comprehensive data sets we have been able to find with those features are in the World Values Surveys (WVS) and European Values Surveys (EVS) with which we can compare citizens' attitudes in 1990 (WVS wave 2, with about 13,000 respondents), 2006 (WVS wave 5, with about 19,000 respondents), and 2018 (EVS wave 5, with about 16,000 respondents) in Britain, France, Germany, Italy, the Netherlands, Norway, Sweden, and the United States. In the following analyses, we use demographic weights for each survey to secure representative samples of the national population.

2.1 Measuring Occupational Groups

Based on self-reported occupation, we assign respondents to occupational groups designed to conform to the influential categories of Oesch (2006) which capture features of the workplace situation said to condition people's views on economic and cultural issues. Because of limitations in the WVS data, we can only approximate those categories, but we do so by grouping people into seven occupational groups according to the types of tasks associated with their employment. These groups are: managers; professionals; high-skill white-collar workers; lower-level service workers; manual workers in crafts and trades; manual production workers; and employers with a small number of employees. The average levels of income and education in each of these occupational groups correspond to our expectations, increasing our confidence in this classification (for details, see Appendix A, Table AA1). Where respondents do not list a present occupation, we use the past occupation they report to assign them to an occupational class; and we drop from the sample those who do not report an occupation.

2.2 Assessing Attitudes

One advantage of the WVS is that attitudes can be measured using the same questions in every wave. We measure citizens' views about economic issues with questions about their attitudes to income inequality; private versus state ownership of business; the responsibility of government to provide for all; whether the unemployed should be forced to take any job; and whether competition is good or harmful. We assess views about cultural issues with questions about whether homosexuality and abortion are justifiable; how respondents feel about having immigrants, Muslims, and people of a different race as neighbors; whether men have more right to a job than women; and whether respect for authority is good or bad. The questions used are in Appendix B.

Using these questions, based on the entire pooled sample, we construct indices for people's views on economic and cultural issues by estimating a confirmatory model for multidimensional item response parameters, based on Samejima's (1969) multidimensional ordinal response model because the data are ordinal (Chalmers 2012). Given our premise that these questions tap two distinct factors, we constrain the variables to load onto one dimension. Our economic index reflects attitudes to redistribution and governmental activism, which we describe as left versus right, while the cultural index reflects a set of values we describe as cosmopolitan versus traditional.[3] Details of the factor analysis are in Appendix C. The cross-national and over-time patterns observed with our measures correspond broadly to those found by Caughey et al. (2019), which enhances our confidence in the results.

2.3 Movements within a Two-Dimensional Electoral Space

Using the average position on economic and cultural issues taken by members of each occupational group, we place these groups within a two-dimensional issue space at three points in time around 1990, 2006, and 2018. The results are reported in Figure 2, which documents the movement of occupational groups across this electoral space over the past three decades within the eight countries examined here. The metric on the axes is based on factor scores calculated over the entire sample and hence comparable across waves. Results for individual countries are reported in Appendix D. Several general features of the movement of these groups are notable.

The first is an important secular development. Over the course of these decades, views about cultural issues across all occupational groups became consistently more cosmopolitan. That movement was especially pronounced between 1990 and 2006 but it continued through 2018; and it is also visible, albeit at different rates, within each of the countries in this study (see Appendix D). At a time when public attention is often fixed on the resistance that populist right politicians have mounted to cosmopolitan cultural views in the name of traditional values, it is worth underlining that the broader and more durable trend within these democracies has been rising support for more cosmopolitan values associated with gender equality, abortion rights, and cultural tolerance.[4]

The movement of people's views on economic issues is equally interesting. Between 1990 and 2006, the views of all occupational groups shifted quite dramatically to the left on economic issues, toward more support for redistribution and state intervention. In the following twelve years between 2006 and

---

[3] Other terms used for a roughly similar cultural spectrum are left-libertarian versus right-authoritarian (cf. Kitschelt 2004) and universalism versus particularism (cf. Häusermann and Kriesi 2015).

[4] It should be noted that cultural views on issues of gender rights, abortion, and the like have been more fluid than those on immigration, which fluctuate to some extent over time but show greater stability (see Caughey et al. 2019).

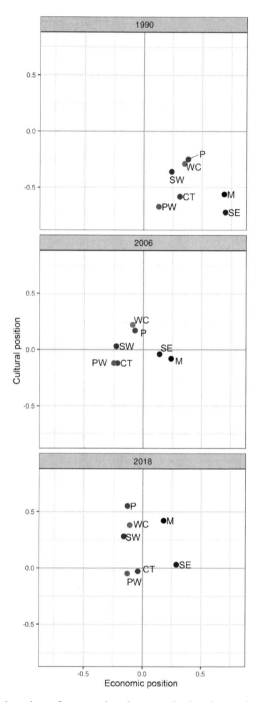

Figure 2 The location of occupational groups in the electoral space in 1990, 2006, and 2018 across all eight countries (average).

Note: M – managers; P – professionals; WC – high-skill white-collar workers; SW – lower-level service workers; SE – small employers; CT – manual crafts and trades workers; PW – manual production workers. For point estimates, see Appendix D.

Source: Authors' calculations from WVS/EVS.

2018, however, we see a bifurcation in views, as lower-level workers and small employers shift to the right again on economic issues, while professionals and skilled white-collar workers remain on the left, and sometimes move slightly further left on economic issues – a development that is consequential for coalition formation (see also Kitschelt and Rehm 2022).

An equally important bifurcation on cultural issues is also evident in the later period. After drawing somewhat more closely together on cultural issues between 1990 and 2006, the positions of some occupational groups diverged dramatically on those issues between 2006 and 2018. The cultural views of professionals, skilled white-collar workers, lower-level service workers, and managers became considerably more cosmopolitan in this period, while the views of production workers, crafts and trades workers, and small employers, on average, did not. As a result, substantial gaps on cultural issues have emerged between most white-collar and blue-collar workers over the past fifteen years.

Despite these general movements, there is a striking stability in the overall positions that occupational groups have held relative to one another in each period. On economic issues, manual production workers and lower-level service workers have generally held the most left-wing economic positions, while managers and small employers anchor the right side of the economic axis. On cultural issues, professionals and skilled white-collar workers have usually had the most cosmopolitan positions, while manual workers and small employers have held more traditional views.

Figure 2 confirms some of the central contentions in the literature about the changing basis for electoral competition. Since 1990, the electoral space has become more fragmented (**H1**). Occupational groups have taken up more divergent positions within this space, especially on cultural issues, ipso facto making it more difficult for political parties to form coalitions that yield governing pluralities or majorities. Measured by standard deviations, the variation in views between occupational groups on economic issues narrowed slightly, from 0.22 to 0.18 between 1990 and 2018, but the variation in their views on cultural issues increased from 0.19 to 0.24 (for details, see Appendix D). However, this fragmentation is largely a development of the past fifteen years: between 1990 and 2006, the views of occupational groups became somewhat more homogenous on both economic and cultural issues.

These figures also confirm the contention (**H2**) that the fragmentation of the electorate is attributable largely to increasing heterogeneity in voters' views on cultural issues. On economic issues, the gap between the occupational groups with the most left-wing and right-wing views fell by 21 percent between 1990 and 2018, while the gap between groups with the most divergent views on cultural issues increased by 28 percent. Parallel developments are also evident

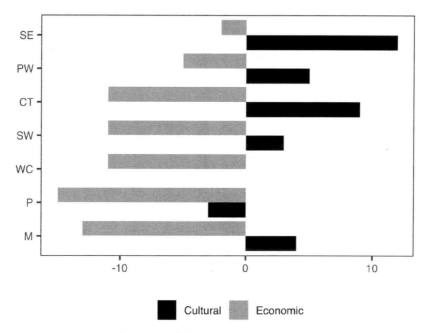

Figure 3 Changes in the standard deviation of views within occupational groups on economic and cultural issues between 1990 and 2018.

Note: Standard deviations multiplied by 100 for clarity of presentation. For labeling of the occupational groups, see Figure 2.

Source: Authors' calculations from WVS/EVS.

within occupational groups. Figure 3 uses the standard deviation for views within each occupational group to indicate how much the variation of views *within* these groups changed between 1990 and 2018. It indicates that, over those years, the variation in people's views on economic issues declined within all occupational groups, but on cultural issues that variation increased within all groups except for professionals and high-skill white-collar workers.

These results are also consistent with the claim (**H3**) that there has been an especially striking divergence in views on cultural issues between blue-collar and white-collar workers. When we compare the average stance taken by manual workers to those taken by skilled white-collar workers and professionals, we find that the gap between them on economic issues has increased by a modest 15 percent, but on cultural issues it increased by 47 percent between 1990 and 2018.

There is mixed support here for the contention that, as the working class has become segmented into groups with different levels of employment security and wages, the views of those groups on economic issues will diverge (**H4**). We cannot fully adjudicate this matter because we lack fine-grained measures for wages and working conditions, and our measure for people's views on economic issues is a relatively general one. But there is some evidence for divisions among the working class on economic issues in the observation that relatively skilled crafts and trades workers consistently hold more right-wing economic views than production workers and lower-level service workers.

Figure 2 indicates that the economic views of all three groups converged to the left during the heyday of liberalization from 1990 to 2006, suggesting that a certain amount of working-class solidarity on economic issues was possible even as dual labor markets grew. In the subsequent decade, however, crafts and trades workers again moved farther to the right than the other two groups on economic issues. To establish whether there are other divisions within the working class, however, we would need more data than we have about the views of various occupational groups regarding specific types of policies, including levels of employment protection, active labor market policies, and various forms of social investment. On specific economic issues such as these, their views might well differ.

What Figure 2 does reveal is an important gap within the working class on cultural issues. Throughout these decades, lower-level service workers display attitudes on cultural issues that are consistently more cosmopolitan than those of production or crafts and trades workers. To some extent, this is to be expected. Kitschelt and Rehm (2014) argue that occupations requiring interpersonal skills, as many lower-level service jobs do, promote more cosmopolitan values. But this is a telling finding. Considerable attention has been devoted to potential gaps across segments of the working class on economic issues. But, in the countries we examine, the working class is even more divided on cultural issues than on economic ones – a divergence likely to have considerable electoral importance (cf. Ares 2017).

2.4 The Wider Context for These Movements

What explains the movements of voters within the electoral space over these three decades? Although it is beyond the scope of this Element to provide full explanations for these movements, which are multiply determined, we want to use the data we have available to situate two of the most dramatic movements in citizens' attitudes over these decades within the context of broader economic and political developments during this time. The first is the widespread movement toward more cosmopolitan values seen in these decades; and the second is the pronounced shift of most occupational groups toward the left on economic issues between 1990 and 2006.

Belying the folk wisdom that, if economic and political circumstances frequently change, "culture" is more stable, the cultural views of all occupational groups became substantially more cosmopolitan during these three decades. Across all the countries we examine, those changes in cultural attitudes were dramatic, especially with respect to issues of gender equality and racial or ethnic tolerance (see also Caughey et al. 2019). Several factors can be said to lie behind this movement.

The first is rising rates of tertiary education. In the countries of the European Union, the share of the working-age population with a tertiary education ranged from less than 10 percent to about 25 percent in 1990, but that range almost doubled to between 20 and 50 percent by 2018 (OECD 2017). In line with this, the average educational level of all occupational groups in our sample increased between 1990 and 2018 (see Appendix A, Table AA1). Increases in rates of higher education matter because the experience of higher education is usually associated with the acquisition of more cosmopolitan attitudes (Weakliem 2002; Scott 2022).

There is some evidence for this in Figure 4, which reports the average economic and cultural views of people from our full sample divided into various sociodemographic groups at each of the three time periods examined (detailed figures are in Appendix I). Higher scores in this figure indicate more conservative economic views and more cosmopolitan cultural views. In Figure 4, the first row compares respondents who have a tertiary education to those who do not. Although there is not much difference in the views of the two groups with respect to economic issues, we see that respondents with a tertiary education have consistently more cosmopolitan cultural attitudes than those with lower levels of educational attainment, and the difference between the two groups grows over time. Because professionals, skilled white-collar workers, and managers are more likely than blue-collar workers or small employers to have a university education (as Appendix A, Table AA1 indicates) – and became more likely over these decades to have a degree as the incidence of tertiary education expanded – differences in rates of tertiary education may also be contributing to the gap in cultural attitudes between these two occupational groups (see also Gethin et al. 2022; Kitschelt and Rehm 2022).

However, this is a context in which gender also matters. Over these years, rising rates of female labor-force participation altered the gender composition of occupational groups, with potential consequences for the cultural attitudes found within them. In the European Union, the share of women in the labor force increased by about 10 percent from just below 42 percent in 1990 to more than 46 percent in 2018. In Figure 4, the second row indicates that women are more likely than men to hold cosmopolitan cultural views – an unsurprising finding given that attitudes toward gender equality at work and the right to abortion are components of that index. Hence, the average attitudes of some

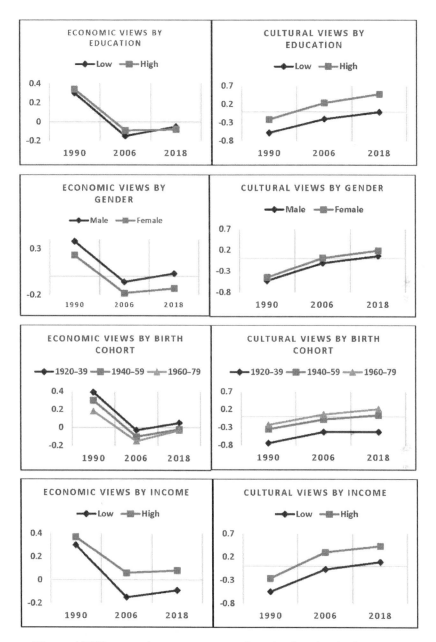

Figure 4 Differences in average economic and cultural attitudes among socioeconomic groups, 1990–2018.

Note: Higher scores indicate more conservative economic views and more cosmopolitan cultural views. High income indicates respondents in the top 30 percent and low income those in the bottom 70 percent of the income distribution. High education indicates people with a tertiary education and low education those without. Cohorts are birth cohorts. For details, see Appendix I.

occupational groups may have become more cosmopolitan as the gender balance of employment within them shifted.

In addition to these composition effects, there is also evidence that the experience of working in paid employment shifts the views of women in cosmopolitan directions; and the experience of working with more women may have altered the views of some men in similar ways (Bolzendahl and Myers 2004).[5] Hence, the feminization of the workforce might have increased the incidence of cosmopolitan cultural attitudes in the workforce; and, since women have moved disproportionately into white-collar and service-sector jobs requiring social skills, this trend may also have contributed to the growing gap on cultural issues between service-sector employees and blue-collar workers.

A third factor shifting values in cosmopolitan directions is generational change. As Mannheim (1952) observed many years ago and Inglehart (1990) has underlined, cultural change often takes place via generational replacement, as older birth cohorts with traditional views are replaced by new cohorts socialized in a different environment. The context in which the younger workers in our sample, born after 1960, were socialized was certainly different from the one experienced by their parents born in the interwar years. Beginning in the 1960s, the pursuit of racial and gender equality became prominent public goals. In subsequent decades, mainstream discourse increasingly embraced social equality, and the practices of many institutions in both Europe and the United States shifted in parallel directions. School textbooks began to put much more emphasis on respect for diversity (Bromley 2009); and multicultural policies have been pursued with more vigor in Europe since 1980 (Banting and Kymlicka 2013).

Hence, as younger workers entered the labor force in recent decades and older workers retired, the cultural views of people in most occupations were likely to have become, on average, more cosmopolitan. In Figure 4, the third row is congruent with these observations. It indicates that people born into more recent birth cohorts hold more cosmopolitan cultural views than their elders, and they continue to do so even as they age. It is notable that the workers most likely to retire over the decades examined here, namely, those born during the interwar years, have consistently held cultural views that are more traditional than those of people in the postwar generations who succeeded them.

As Norris and Inglehart (2019) note, however, there may also be an endogenous dynamic to these developments that intensifies cultural conflict. They argue that the growing cosmopolitanism of an increasingly educated elite can inspire

---

[5] Note that the evidence on these matters is mixed (Andersen and Cook 1985; Banaszak and Plutzer 1993), and in some cases the experience of working with women may reinforce the traditional values of some men (cf. Kimmel 2013; Gidron and Hall 2017). This subject merits more research.

people in less-privileged socioeconomic positions to mount a stronger defense of traditional values. That type of backlash is understandable. As the anthropologist Margaret Mead once observed, in contexts of rapid social change, people often feel like immigrants in their own land; and that feeling is currently palpable among some social groups who feel "left behind" by contemporary developments (Eribon 2013; Hochschild 2016; Gidron and Hall 2017). Although all occupational groups adopted more cosmopolitan views over these decades, if there is a backlash, we should expect them to do so at different rates. And that is what we find. As Figure 2 indicates, educated professionals, managers, and skilled white-collar workers have generally embraced highly cosmopolitan values, but the views of many blue-collar workers and small employers shifted more slowly. In keeping with this, the first row in Figure 4 indicates that the gap on cultural issues between people with and without a college education grew by about 30 percent between 1990 and 2018.

Although broad socioeconomic developments of the sort we have just cited are important, they are rarely the only factors behind large-scale shifts in attitudes. Politics also matters (Evans and Tilley 2011, 2017). In this case, the support that mainstream politicians have offered for cosmopolitan values has helped to diffuse them, while the backlash against them has been fueled by the defense of traditional values used by entrepreneurial politicians to mobilize electoral support on the populist right (Hobolt and De Vries 2020). That clash has increased the salience of cultural issues to electoral politics and intensified social conflict between the groups that embrace cosmopolitan and traditional values. In elegant work, Ares (2022) shows that the attitudes of people in different occupational classes concerning economic and cultural issues are more likely to diverge when political parties politicize the relevant issues. In sum, although the movements in cultural views documented here are rooted in socioeconomic developments, they have been amplified by the rhetoric of rival contenders for political power.

The second pronounced shift in attitudes over this period that demands explanation is the wholesale shift to the left in the views of citizens on economic issues between 1990 and 2006. In those years, all occupational groups became more hostile to market competition, more supportive of income redistribution, and more willing to say that governments should ensure that everyone is provided for (see Appendix B). Understanding the factors behind this movement in public opinion takes us into different terrain but, once again, both socioeconomic developments and political factors play prominent roles.

In many respects, it is not surprising that people's economic views should shift to the left during this time because these were years when economic developments were combining to eliminate decent middle-skill jobs, increase income inequality, and render employment more precarious for many people. These developments have been well-documented elsewhere (Glyn 2006; Baccaro and Howell 2017). Their origins lie in changes in the strategies of firms that led to the outsourcing and offshoring of jobs, the replacement of long-term employment contracts with temporary ones, higher levels of income inequality, and the growth of secondary labor markets featuring lower wages, fewer benefits, and little employment security (Hall 2022b). Many of these shifts in firm strategy were responses to the liberalization of finance, the globalization of world markets, the expansion of a single European market, and skill-biased technological change (Goos et al. 2009; Palier and Thelen 2010; Emmenger et al. 2012; Hall 2022a,).

Of course, lower-income groups generally suffered more from these economic developments than others and, if their adverse effects were responsible for shifting people's economic views to the left, we should see a more pronounced movement among lower-income groups (Rommel and Walter 2018). There is evidence for that in the bottom row of Figure 4, which indicates that lower-income workers moved more sharply to the left on economic issues over these years than people with higher levels of income.

It is notable, however, that this response was not restricted to lower-income groups. The economic views of workers in all occupations moved to the left during the 1990s, including people who were in a better position to take advantage of globalized markets. How is this to be explained? Shifts in the character of the occupational structure that left many people in more vulnerable positions are likely to have played a role. As tertiary education expanded, holding a college degree no longer guaranteed people a high income or secure job (Autor et al. 2020; Schwander 2020). Many college graduates began to have difficulty finding jobs commensurate with their skills and expectations (Ansell and Gingrich 2021). Some white-collar jobs were threatened by increasingly sophisticated forms of automation (Peugny 2019). As a result, compared to prior decades, many people with relatively high levels of education and white-collar jobs had only middling incomes and more exposure to the economic turbulence of this period. These developments may help to explain why the views of many professionals and high-skilled white-collar workers on economic issues moved to the left during the 1990s and early 2000s, and also why many of them retained such views through 2018 (see also Kitschelt and Rehm 2022).

Of course, the other set of developments likely to have pushed people's economic views to the left during the 1990s were the neoliberal policies that many governments pursued in those years. Those policies liberalized labor markets, reduced employment protection, privatized public enterprises, rendered many jobs less secure, and intensified competition across sectors, thereby putting pressure on firms to reduce their labor costs. Although social spending continued to rise, governments cut back the generosity of social benefits and many began to tie the receipt of social benefits to a willingness to take low-paid jobs (for overviews, see Peck 2001; Pierson 2001; Dolvik and Martin 2015). These developments, too, are well-documented (see Centeno and Cohen 2012; Schmidt and Thatcher 2014).

Neoliberal policies complemented the strategies of firms during this era, but they also magnified the adverse effects of those strategies, increasing income inequality and rendering the livelihoods of many people more insecure (Hall 2022b). More evidence would be needed to establish that the neoliberal policies of this era pushed people's economic views toward the left during the 1990s. But at least three considerations point in that direction. First, this movement in public opinion corresponds to the well-established observation associated with "thermostatic" images of politics that when governments move strongly in one direction – in this case to the right on economic issues – the views of citizens on those issues tend to move in the opposite direction (Soroka and Wlezien 2010). Second, these policies exposed many people to higher levels of labor market risk, and there is evidence that exposure to labor market risk increases support for social protection (Rehm 2016). Third, the timing of this shift in people's stance on economic issues coincides with the implementation of neoliberal policies. Although parallel policies were initiated a decade earlier in the United States and Britain, neoliberal reform in Europe took place primarily during the 1990s and reached its apogee on both continents during that decade (Fill 2019). Accordingly, we would expect the backlash against it to be concentrated in those years.

More research leveraging cross-national variation would be required to identify just what shifted public opinion during this era. We have been able to sketch only some of the relevant developments. But we turn now to two other factors central to the nature of electoral competition in these decades, namely, the movement of political parties within the electoral space and important shifts in the relative salience of economic and cultural issues.

3 Party Strategies and Issue Salience

To assess the next set of contentions about the rise of challenger parties and the decline of mainstream parties, we need to consider how political parties moved within this electoral space in these eight countries and whether there were shifts in the electoral salience of cultural versus economic issues. As noted, some scholars have argued that rising support for populist parties was largely a reaction against the convergence of mainstream parties on economic issues during the 1990s and early 2000s by voters seeking policies that mainstream parties no longer offered (**H5**). Did party platforms converge in those years? Were the positions taken by mainstream parties in this period unrepresentative of the views of major segments of the electorate?

3.1 Party Strategies

To position political parties in a comparable electoral space, we use the Manifesto Project (MP) dataset (Volkens et al. 2018). Compared to expert surveys, it has the advantages of covering the entire time period we examine and of yielding measures based on the actual positions taken by parties in their electoral manifestos without any biases that expert evaluations might introduce. Parties generally seem to pursue the policies outlined in their manifestos (Thomson et al. 2017). To measure party positions on each dimension, we use all the items in the MP dataset that cover the entire period and are clearly relevant. To assess the positions of parties on economic issues, we use positive references to Keynesian demand management, nationalization, welfare state expansion, and labor groups to indicate left positions; and we take positive references to a free market economy, market deregulation, limitations on the welfare state, and negative references to labor groups to indicate right positions. To assess the positions of parties on the cultural dimension, we use positive references to multiculturalism and underprivileged minority groups and negative references to nationalism and traditional morality to indicate cosmopolitan positions; and we take negative references to multiculturalism and positive references to nationalism and traditional morality to indicate more traditional views.

We aggregate these variables into indices for each party's position on economic and cultural issues following the widely used procedure of Lowe et al. (2011) based on logit scores. Compared to an approach that uses additive scales, this has the advantages that only variables associated with economic or cultural issues influence the estimated position of a party on economic or cultural issues, respectively, and the contribution each additional sentence on a topic makes to the construction of the scale is weighted by reference to how many other sentences already address that topic (details in Appendix E).

Aggregating across our eight countries, Figure 5 shows the positions of the principal party families in this electoral space in 1990–1 (panel a), 2006–9 (panel b), and 2017–18 (panel c). The metric on the axes is scores on the two indices standardized with the mean and standard deviation of the 1990 sample. Although the electoral space in which we place parties is not identical to the one in which we place citizens, because the items used to measure positions on

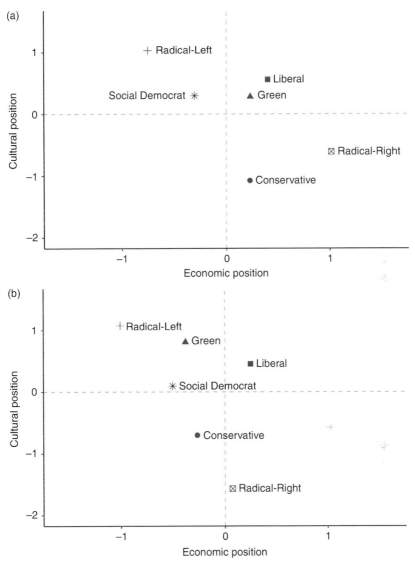

Figure 5 Positions of party families in the electoral space

Note: Panel (a) – circa 1990–1; panel (b) – circa 2006–9; panel (c) – circa 2018. Calculated from Manifesto Project data for the eight countries in this study. The term 'Conservative' refers to all center-right parties and 'Social Democrat' to all center-left parties.

cultural and economic issues for parties and citizens are not the same, the two spaces are roughly commensurable for capturing broad positions on the issues on which we focus and for comparing the direction of movement over time by parties and voters.

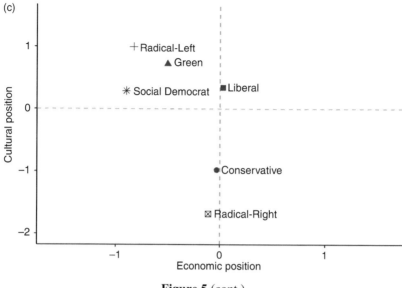

Figure 5 (cont.)

As a check on these conclusions, we use the schema devised by Wagner and Meyer (2017) to group parties into the categories of mainstream left, mainstream right, and radical-right and examine the movement of these party families in this issue space across all eight countries over the period between 1990 and 2018. Those results are in Figure 6.

Figure 5 confirms that the positions of most parties, including mainstream center-left and center-right parties, did converge on economic issues during the 1990s and early 2000s. Panel (a) of the Figure shows that in 1990–1 the principal party families were located along a diagonal running from the northwest (NW) to the southeast (SE) quadrants of the electoral space (see also Kriesi et al. 2006). By 2006–9, however, the economic platforms of most parties had converged, and the axis of partisan competition shifted toward the vertical, reducing competition on economic issues in favor of competition on cultural issues (see also Kitschelt 2004).

However, the movements of political parties on economic issues within these countries do not entirely conform to those expected by analysts who explain rising support for populist parties as a response to this movement. As those analysts claim, the economic positions of mainstream parties did converge. But those accounts generally emphasize the importance of a movement by social democratic parties toward the right on economic issues, of the sort associated with "Third Way" social democracy, whereas the convergence in mainstream party positions between 1990 and 2006 that we observe is marked mainly by the

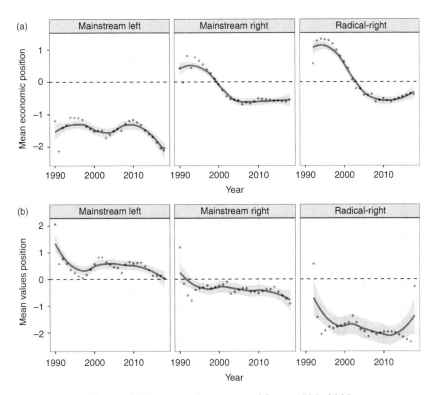

Figure 6 Movement in party positions, 1990–2020

Note: Panel (a) – movement on economic issues; panel (b) – movement on cultural issues. Scatter plot and Loess smoothed curve for mean party family position on economic and cultural indices. Metric on y-axis is number of standard deviations above or below the 1990 mean in the sample. Higher scores indicate more right-wing positions on economic issues and more cosmopolitan positions on cultural issues.

Source: Manifesto Project.

movement of conservative parties to the economic left. Moreover, in the subsequent decade, social democratic parties moved even farther left, offering platforms more distinctive from those of conservative parties. These movements call into question the contention that rising support for radical parties can be attributed to the convergence of center-left parties on neoliberal economic policies (**H5**).

Similarly, there is little evidence here to support the claim that the movement of center-left parties toward more cosmopolitan positions on cultural issues ignited a reaction yielding increased support for right populist parties (**H6**). Populist right parties gained support most rapidly during the late 1990s and 2000s, but the position of social democratic parties on cultural issues changed very little over this period, and some parties moved in slightly traditional directions. Between 1990 and 2006, Green parties adopted significantly more cosmopolitan cultural positions, but the overall stance of mainstream parties barely changed. Far more notable for the purpose of explaining rising support for radical-right parties is the movement of radical-right parties to the left on economic issues between 1990 and 2018. Parties that had once been focused on reducing levels of taxation and public expenditure became much more support-ive of social protection, especially in the form of income maintenance programs such as unemployment insurance and public pensions (Lefkofridi and Michel 2017). As a result, radical-right parties were now more attractive to many working-class voters (Lefkofridi et al. 2014; Harteveld 2016; Rovny and Polk 2019b).

From a broader perspective, however, there are failures of representation here that may account for the alienation of some key groups of voters and an associated decline in the electoral support given to mainstream political parties, especially on the center-left. These failures are visible if we compare Figure 2, which shows the positions of citizens in various occupational groups within the electoral space, and Figure 5 which displays the positions taken by political parties in that space. We see that the economic platforms of most parties shifted somewhat to the left between 1990 and 2006, in line with the movement of most citizens during those years. That shift suggests a modest responsiveness to the median voter. But when we look at the positions of specific occupational groups, the picture is less rosy. As Figure 2 indicates, workers in production and crafts and trades, who typically make up more than a third of the national workforce, have generally held relatively left-wing views on economic issues and trad-itional views on cultural issues, which place them in the southwest quadrant of the electoral space by 2006. Yet throughout these decades, there were no parties centrally placed in that part of the electoral space speaking for both the economic and cultural views of those workers. Thus, there are good reasons for thinking that many people in the working-class may have felt alienated from mainstream electoral politics and, hence, open to the appeals of anti-establish-ment contenders (Van der Brug and van Spanje 2009; Evans and Hall 2019; Hillen and Steiner 2020).

There is some evidence for such alienation in Table 1 which reports the percentage of people saying they are "very interested" or "somewhat interested" in politics (compared with "not very interested" or "not at all interested") at each of the three points in time indicated. Not surprisingly, professionals and man-agers are consistently more interested in politics than people in other occupa-tional groups; but, throughout the period, the majority of production workers expressed little interest in politics. The changes over time are also telling. Interest in politics fell among all occupational groups between 1990 and

Table 1 Percentage of each occupational group expressing interest in politics

	1990	2006	2018	Change
Professionals	71	74	62	- 13%
Managers	71	59	61	- 14%
Small employers	62	58	55	- 12%
Skilled white-collar workers	61	65	46	- 25%
Crafts and trades workers	58	49	42	- 28%
Low-skilled service workers	57	51	41	- 28%
Production workers	43	38	39	- 9%

Source: WVS/EVS.

2018, but it fell especially sharply among crafts and trades workers and low-skilled service workers, and perhaps less sharply among production workers only because their interest in politics was already so low. By 2018, about 60 percent of workers in production, crafts and trades, and lower-level services were expressing little or no interest in politics.

The rhetoric of many politicians on the radical-right and radical-left exploited this type of alienation, by emphasizing that their parties would speak for people whom the mainstream parties were ignoring (Berger 2017; Grzymala-Busse 2019). As radical-right parties moved toward the center on economic issues and toward even more traditional stances on cultural issues, they could make such appeals with growing credibility; and there is evidence that those appeals were effective in the fact that many of the voters recruited by populist parties were previously nonvoters (Abou-Chadi et al. 2021; Silva and Wratil 2023).

3.2 Issue Salience

Many observers have noted that populist right parties base their appeals to voters primarily on cultural rather than economic issues, with special emphasis on the cultural threats putatively posed by immigrants (Ivarsflaten 2008; Rovny and Polk 2019b). Therefore, rising support for populist right parties and falling support for mainstream parties may be attributable, at least in part, to an increase in the electoral salience of cultural issues relative to economic issues (**H7**). As Oesch and Rennwald (2018:14) argue, "depending on whether economic or cultural issues are more salient, production and service workers either choose the left or the radical right."

To assess this contention, in Figure 7 we report changes in the proportions of party manifestos devoted to cultural and economic issues in the eight democracies over the postwar period, weighted by the share of votes secured by each

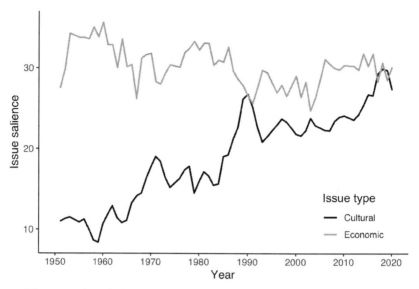

Figure 7 The relative salience of economic and cultural issues in party
platforms

Note: Calculated from Manifesto Project data. For the construction of the categories, see
Appendix F.

party (details in Appendix F). This measure is widely considered a good
indicator for the salience of different types of issues to electoral competition.
It indicates that economic issues continued to command attention throughout
these decades, and their salience rose during the major recessions of the 1970s
and 2008–9. But the salience of cultural issues increased dramatically during
the 1980s and again after 2006. In 2018, economic and cultural issues were
equally salient to electoral competition in these countries. These figures correspond to the finding of Häusermann and Kriesi (2015) that, by this time, support
for many European political parties was more closely associated with voters'
positions on cultural rather than economic issues (see also Lachat 2008).

To supplement these aggregate figures, Appendix F reports changes in the
relative salience of economic and cultural issues within each of the eight countries
we examine. In general, national trends conform to those visible in Figure 7. In all
these countries, economic issues remain salient, but the relative salience of
cultural issues rises dramatically. The two types of issues reach roughly equal
levels of salience relatively early in the United States, Sweden, and the
Netherlands, but in Italy, Britain, and Norway, where the salience of economic
issues rises especially dramatically after the 2008–9 recession, the importance of
economic issues continues to outstrip cultural issues by some margin.

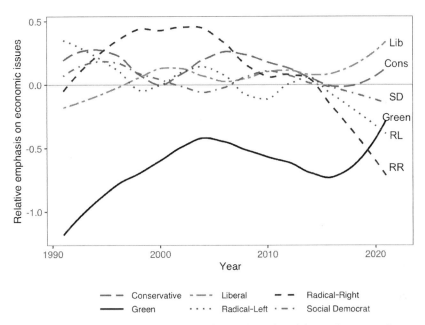

Figure 8 Relative emphasis on economic versus cultural issues by type of party

In many respects, the rising salience of cultural issues is not unexpected. To attract votes, political parties have to offer something distinctive to the electorate. When party platforms converge on economic issues, as they did during the 1990s and early 2000s, political parties seek a different basis on which to distinguish themselves from their opponents and appeals on cultural issues proved to be an attractive alternative (Hobolt and De Vries 2020). However, some parties shifted their emphasis toward cultural issues more dramatically than others – with implications for how effective their electoral appeals were likely to be. Figure 8 displays changes in the balance of emphasis in the platforms of party families since 1990.[6] We can see that liberal, social democratic, and conservative parties continued to give more prominence to economic issues, compared to radical-right, radical-left, and Green parties which put more emphasis on cultural issues. In a context where cultural issues were increasingly central to partisan competition, that may have placed mainstream parties at an electoral disadvantage vis-à-vis their challengers.

Figure 7 provides us with a good sense of how salient economic and cultural issues have been to overall partisan competition. But we would also like to

---

[6] The measures for Figure 8 are based on the sum of the variables used to measure a party's position on economic issues divided by the sum of the variables used to calculate a party's position on cultural issues using the items from the Manifesto Project detailed in Appendix F. We interpolate scores for each party between election years and take the mean by party family across all eight countries for each year. The scores are then standardized.

assess how important economic versus cultural issues were to the political behavior of individual voters during these years. To do so, we take people's interest in politics as a proxy for their political engagement. With OLS regressions, we estimate how strong the relationship is between people's views on economic and cultural issues and their interest in politics. On the premise that people with a greater interest in politics are more likely to vote, this estimation should be informative about what types of issues are more likely to influence people's votes. Our dependent variable is "interest in politics" measured on a four-point scale, as in Table 1. The explanatory variables of interest are indices assessing a respondent's views about economic and cultural issues, standardized to be comparable. We also condition the estimation on a set of other variables known to affect interest in politics – levels of education and income, gender, and age, all of which show associations in the expected direction in the resulting estimation – and we include country and wave fixed effects. Because we use absolute values for the indices measuring attitudes, the coefficients on those variables indicate whether holding strong views on those issues in either direction is associated with higher levels of interest in politics.

Figure 9 reports results for the entire cross-national sample in each wave. The relevant coefficients suggest that economic issues have been closely associated

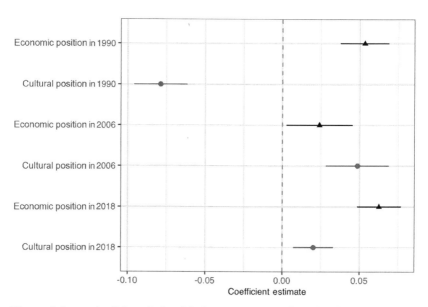

Figure 9 Strength of the relationship between economic and cultural views and interest in politics across waves in the cross-national sample.

Source: WVS/EVS.

with people's interest in politics throughout the entire period, reflecting their overall salience to partisan competition visible in Figure 7. But these results also indicate that the political salience of cultural issues increased over these decades. In 1990, people with strong views on cultural issues were unlikely to be interested in politics. By 2006, however, those who held strong views about cultural issues were at least as likely as people with strong views about economic issues to be interested in politics; and, although economic issues again assumed importance in 2018, strong views on both types of issues were associated with interest in politics.

Table 2 provides parallel results for each of the seven occupational groups in the analysis. Although the coefficients in the table should be treated with caution because the small sample size for some occupations limits their statistical significance, positive coefficients indicate that people in that occupational group who held strong views on the relevant set of issues were more likely to be interested in politics than others in that occupational group, while negative coefficients indicate that people in that group with strong views on the issues were less likely than others to be interested in politics. The absence of a coefficient indicates that strong views on the relevant set of issues were not associated with interest in politics among that occupational group.

Table 2 Relationship between economic and cultural views and interest in politics among occupational groups

Occupation	M	P	WC	SW	CT	PW	SE
1990							
Economic	–	0.07	–	0.06	0.03	0.09	0.05*
Cultural	–	–	–	–	- 0.11	- 0.09	- 0.07**
2006							
Economic	–	0.07	0.09	–	–	–	–
Cultural	–	0.05	0.06**	0.05**	–	–	–
2018							
Economic	–	0.12	0.06	0.07	0.07	–	–
Cultural	–	0.06	0.11	0.05	- 0.06**	–	-0.08**

Source: WVS/EVS surveys.

Notes: For the occupational categories, see Figure 2. All coefficients are statistically significant at the $p < 0.01$ level except ** is $p < 0.05$ and * is $p < 0.10$.

Table 2 suggests that in 1990 economic issues inspired interest in politics among people in most occupational groups, but cultural issues did not. Indeed, blue-collar workers and small employers with strong views on cultural issues in 1990 tended to be uninterested in politics. By 2018, however, economic issues still inspired interest in politics among most groups, but strong views on cultural issues were also closely associated with interest in politics among three occupational groups – professionals, white-collar employees, and lower-level service workers. These results confirm that, although economic issues remained salient, cultural issues became increasingly salient to political engagement over these decades. Moreover, the people whose views on cultural issues were most likely to inspire political engagement were those working in service-related occupations. By contrast, the stronger the views of blue-collar workers and small employers on cultural issues, the less likely they were to be interested in politics – perhaps a reflection of the levels of political alienation visible in Table 1.

Another approach to assessing the salience of economic and cultural issues to political behavior is to examine how closely related people's views about such issues are to their votes for specific types of parties (Häusermann and Kriesi 2015; Polk and Rovny 2018). We do so with logistic regressions on the entire sample where the dependent variable is the vote for each of five party families – center-left, center-right, radical-left, radical-right, and Green parties – and the coefficients of interest are those on indices for the respondent's economic and cultural views standardized for the sake of comparability. We condition this estimation on several other variables likely to affect a person's vote – age, gender, level of education and income – and include fixed effects for countries and waves. The results for 1990 and 2018 are in Table AF1 in Appendix F.

As might be expected from our findings based on party manifestos displayed in Figure 7, economic and cultural issues appear to be highly salient to voting behavior in both periods. People's views about both types of issues are associated with their votes for all party families in 1990 and 2018 at high levels of statistical significance. The relative strength of the association between people's economic, as compared to their cultural, views and their votes increases over these years for all types of parties, except the radical-right; and that yields some anticipated variation in which issues matter more to the voters for each political party. In 2018, voting for center-left, center-right, and radical-left parties is more closely associated with their supporters' views on economic issues than with their views on cultural issues, while support for Green and radical-right parties is more strongly associated with their voters' views on cultural issues. The general picture that emerges from this estimation is one of an electoral arena in which economic and cultural issues are both salient to voting behavior, although economic issues tend to draw voters to center-left and radical-left parties, while cultural issues are more important to the appeal of radical-right and Green parties and, to some extent, center-right parties.

4 Assessing the Viability of Electoral Coalitions

Building on these analyses of the movement of voters in the electoral space and shifts in the salience of issues, we turn now to the problem of assessing the relative viability of the electoral coalitions underpinning mainstream center-left and center-right parties vis-à-vis their principal challengers, and how that has changed over the past three decades, with a view to pinpointing some of the factors that may lie behind these changes.

4.1 Identifying Feasible Coalitions

As noted, we consider coalitions composed of voters grouped by occupation, and we concentrate on four potential coalitions corresponding to those that center-left, center-right, Green, and radical-right parties can be expected to try to assemble. For the purposes of this analysis, we specify that each coalition must include substantial support from three occupational groups. Rarely can a party secure a dominant position in the legislature without considerable support from at least three groups, although some parties may command support from more than three groups. All the coalitions considered here encompass occupational groups representing at least a third of the electorate, the minimum share of the vote needed to dominate a coalition government in this era (see Armingeon et al. 2019), and in most cases they represent 40 percent of the electorate or more.

We focus on the electoral coalitions that these four types of parties have actually tried to assemble. Accordingly, our specifications for the occupational groups to be included in the core coalition assembled by each type of party are based on empirical findings from recent studies of partisan support, which broadly agree about the occupational groups most likely to vote for each type of party (Oesch 2008a, 2008b; Geering and Häusermann 2013; Häusermann and Kriesi 2015; Gingrich 2017; Knutsen 2018).

The coalition we term center-left is composed of professionals, skilled white-collar workers, and higher-level manual workers in crafts and trades. This specification reflects the fact that social democratic parties now draw a majority of their votes from middle-class groups (Gingrich and Häusermann 2015; Häusermann 2018) but try to assemble coalitions extending into the working class, where higher levels of unionization among skilled manual workers usually render them the most promising coalition partner (Knutsen

2006; Mosimann and Pontusson 2017). The center-right coalition we consider is composed of professionals, skilled white-collar workers, and small employers. Center-right parties are unlikely to gain enough votes to dominate a legislature unless they secure substantial support from these two middle-class groups as well as small employers. An alternative formulation would include managers in lieu of small employers, but the latter form a larger segment of the electorate in our sample, and they are even more likely than managers to support the center-right (Oesch 2008a). For these reasons, Oesch and Rennwald (2018) identify small employers as the key swing group between the center-right and the radical-right.

We define the radical-right coalition as one assembling support from manual workers in crafts and trades, manual production workers, and small employers, in line with studies indicating that these are the occupational groups most likely to support contemporary radical-right parties (Bornschier and Kriesi 2013; Oesch and Rennwald 2018; Gidron and Hall 2019). Finally, we identify a fourth coalition, which we label a cosmopolitan coalition, joining professionals and skilled white-collar employees to low-skilled service workers, on the premise that shared cultural outlooks among people working in services may make it a viable coalition, especially when the salience of cultural issues is high (Kitschelt and Rehm 2014). We see this as the type of coalition that underpins Green parties or coalition governments composed of Green parties and center-left parties (Rüdig et al. 1991; Dolezal 2010).

Note that we do not consider an electoral coalition composed entirely from the working class, which would join crafts and trade workers, production workers, and lower-level service employees. Although some people would like to see such a party contend for power, our focus is on the coalitions actually assembled by existing parties, and no prominent party family does that in our country cases. The parties that come closest to doing so are radical-left parties, but those parties all draw substantial support from middle-class groups, thereby building electoral coalitions very similar to those of the center-left.

Of course, this exercise is to some extent stylized. The composition of the coalitions formed by individual parties varies to some degree across countries and time, and all parties draw at least some votes from individuals across a wider set of occupations. In some cases, our analysis accommodates that possibility because occupational groups with intermediate views fall within the electoral space circumscribed by the three coalition partners on which we concentrate. However, our specifications generally reflect the occupational groups that are at the core of the coalitions assembled by each type of party; and, in robustness tests, we consider coalitions with different compositions that are the most feasible alternatives to those outlined here.

4.2 Our Approach to Assessing the Viability of Coalitions

To assess the relative viability of coalitions, we adopt a standard spatial analysis based on the ideal points of occupational groups measured in terms of the average position on economic and cultural issues taken by their members (Adams et al. 2005; McDonald and Budge 2005). We assume that parties offer a common program to the electorate. Of course, this is a simplifying assumption: parties sometimes emphasize different appeals when communicating with specific groups of voters, hoping to assemble coalitions on a logrolling basis. But our assumption accords with studies pointing to the nationalization of party politics; and it is realistic in an era when parties publish national manifestos and rely heavily on widespread media coverage (Caramani 2009; Hopkins 2018).

In this context, the more similar the political attitudes of each occupational group to those of other groups in the potential coalition, the easier it will be for a party to assemble support from these groups. Therefore, our measure for the viability of a coalition is the maximum distance in the electoral space that must be spanned if the coalition is to be assembled, i.e. the distance between the groups in each coalition that are the most distant from one another. In the terms of spatial voting models, the smaller that distance, the closer the position of the party can be to the ideal points of all members of the coalition, and hence the more readily they can be rallied around it.

To account for shifts in the relative salience of economic and cultural issues, we consider three scenarios: (1) when economic issues dominate electoral competition; (2) when cultural issues dominate; and (3) when voters accord economic and cultural issues roughly equal weight. We construe salience as a general feature of electoral competition at a given point in time – what Meyer and Wagner (2020) term "systemic salience" (for a review of this issue, see Dennison 2019). Therefore, when electoral competition turns primarily on economic or cultural issues, the relative viability of coalitions will depend on the distance that each coalition spans along the axis in the electoral space that reflects the type of issue specified as dominant. However, our results remain informative if salience is seen as a feature of coalitions rather than of electoral competition. In such cases, the electoral viability of a coalition depends on the maximum distance the coalition spans along the axis most salient to its supporters.

To assess the viability of a coalition in contexts where economic and cultural issues are equally salient to electoral competition, we use the triangle formed when the positions of the three occupational groups in that coalition are joined within this two-dimensional space. The smaller the triangle, the more feasible it should be to form a coalition among the groups; and to measure the size of each triangle we calculate its centroid, namely, the point at which lines joining each vertex with the midpoint of the opposite side intersect, and then sum the distances between the centroid and the vertices. The smaller this sum, the closer the three groups at the points of the triangle are to each other in the electoral space, and the more feasible it should be to form a coalition among them. We label this sum the "size" of the triangle.

4.3 Empirical Results

Using this approach and the positions within the electoral space of the occupational groups in the full cross-national sample displayed in Figure 2, we report, in Table 3, the relevant coalitions, their share of the workforce, and our measures for the viability of each type of coalition in 1990, 2006, and 2018 under three scenarios that are based on the relative salience of economic and cultural issues. When economic issues dominate electoral competition, the relevant measure for the viability of a coalition is the distance separating the groups in it that are farthest apart on the economic axis (column 4). The corresponding measure for the viability of a coalition when cultural issues are dominant is in column 5. When economic and cultural issues are equally salient to electoral competition, the relevant measure is the size of the triangle joining the groups in each coalition (column 6). The smaller the number for the distance in the electoral space a coalition must span, the more viable that coalition is. In each column, the figure for the coalition that emerges as most viable is underlined and in bold.

The results reported in Table 3 yield several conclusions. First, it is apparent that the viability of most types of coalitions turns on the relative salience of economic versus cultural issues. When economic issues dominate electoral competition (column 4), mainstream coalitions, especially of the center-left, do relatively well and the radical-right coalition is the least viable. Conversely, when cultural issues dominate, the radical-right coalition does much better and is often the most viable coalition (column 5). When economic and cultural issues are equally salient (column 6), the coalition that emerges as most viable is the cosmopolitan coalition that Green parties, often in combination with center-left parties, attempt to assemble.

In short, this analysis confirms the contention that radical-right parties are likely to benefit from developments that increase the salience of cultural issues relative to economic ones; and it and suggests that the steady rise in the salience of such issues visible in Figure 7 helps to explain recent increases in support for those parties (**H7**). However, it is notable that, when economic and cultural

Table 3 Coalition potential in 1990, 2006, and 2018 for all countries

Coalition	Composition	Workforce share	Max Distance Economic Axis	Max Distance Cultural Axis	Triangle Size
1990					
Center-left	P + WC + CT	51%	*7*	33	42
Center-right	P + WC + SE	38%	35	47	75
Cosmopolitan	P + WC + SW	47%	14	*11*	*21*
Radical-right	CT + PW + SE	50%	57	14	68
2006					
Center-left	P + WC + CT	52%	*15*	34	46
Center-right	P + WC + SE	38%	23	26	43
Cosmopolitan	P + WC + SW	49%	16	19	*31*
Radical-right	CT + PW + SE	47%	39	*8*	51
2018					
Center-left	P + WC + CT	48%	9	58	67
Center-right	P + WC + SE	43%	42	52	81
Cosmopolitan	P+ WC + SW	67%	*5*	27	*31*
Radical-right	CT + PW + SE	41%	42	*8*	51

Note: All distances in units multiplied by 100. Workforce share is based on the proportion of workers in each occupation in the weighted WVS/EVS sample. The most viable coalitions are in ***bold***. Occupations are: M – managers; P – professionals; WC – skilled white-collar workers; SW –lower-level service workers; SE – small employers; CT – manual crafts and trades workers; PW – manual production workers. Because the groups forming the radical-right coalition are underrepresented in the EVS sample, the workforce share reported for that coalition in 2018 is an average from national labor force figures.

issues are equally salient, a cosmopolitan coalition of service-sector workers of the sort often assembled by Green parties and center-left parties also does well – an especially important observation given that Figure 7 suggests that economic and cultural issues have roughly equal salience in Western democracies today.

Second, these results show that the viability of alternative coalitions is affected not only by changes in issue salience, but also by the movements of social groups within the electoral space. Comparing the distances associated with each coalition in Table 3 with the movement of occupational groups displayed in Figure 2 is illuminating. Between 1990 and 2006, the challenges facing the center-left increased because manual workers moved far enough left on economic issues to make it more difficult for those parties to sustain coalitions combining professionals and skilled white-collar workers with segments of the manual working class. Over the same period, the viability of center-right coalitions (indicated by the distance they would have to span under any of these three scenarios of salience) improved, because the cultural views of small employers became more cosmopolitan and their economic views more centrist.

By 2018, however, the problem for the center-left was no longer primarily divisions among its constituent groups on economic issues, but an increasing gap between white-collar and blue-collar workers on cultural issues. Center-right parties also had more difficulty rallying support because of increasing divisions between the views of their middle-class constituents and small employers on both economic and cultural issues. Looking down the columns in Table 3, when we compare the distances that parties had to span to construct their coalitions in 1990 and 2018, we see that, regardless of which issues were most salient, coalition formation became more difficult for mainstream parties, especially on the center-left, because their constituent groups of voters had moved farther apart in the issue space. Conversely, coalition formation became somewhat easier for the radical-right.

The prospects for the radical-right certainly improve when cultural issues become more salient, and considerable scholarly attention has been paid to those prospects. But, as Figure 7 indicates, the scenario that best describes the current situation in most of these democracies is the one reflected in the last column of Table 3, because economic and cultural issues are now equally salient to electoral politics. And, in that context, one of the most notable features of these results is how auspicious the prospects currently are for what we have termed a cosmopolitan coalition of the sort assembled from the service sector by Green parties in tandem with center-left parties. When economic and cultural issues are equally salient, it is consistently the most viable coalition, confirming the views of scholars who argue that the future of the left lies in such coalitions (Abou-Chadi et al. 2021; Häusermann and Kitschelt 2023).

Figure 2 suggests that the viability of this cosmopolitan coalition stems, first, from the growing attachment of employees in white-collar work or various kinds of service positions to cosmopolitan cultural values. One of the key features of the electoral space in 2018 is how cosmopolitan even lower-level service workers are on cultural issues compared to manual workers. But the viability of this cosmo-politan coalition also seems to depend on another striking feature of the contem-porary electoral space, namely, the willingness of professionals and white-collar workers to embrace more egalitarian economic policies. It may be that the future of the center-left rests on its capacities to assemble coalitions drawn largely from the service sector (see also Kitschelt and Rehm 2022).

These results also offer some support for the contention that the new fulcrum for electoral politics is competition between Green parties, sometimes in com-bination with center-left parties, and radical-right parties, sometimes in alli-ances with the center-right (Kriesi et al. 2006, 2008; Häusermann and Kriesi 2015; Hooghe and Marks 2018; Marks et al. 2021) (**H8**). As Figure 5 indicates, since the early 2000s, partisan competition in these eight countries has been taking place largely along a diagonal axis cutting across the electoral space, anchored at one end by Green parties and at the other by radical-right parties. This is a contest in which cultural divisions are more prominent than economic ones.

In Table 3, the figures at the bottom of column 6 support this portrait of contemporary electoral competition. They indicate that, when economic and cultural issues have roughly equal salience, as they do today, and occupational groups are positioned within the electoral space as they were in 2018, the two most viable electoral coalitions are the cosmopolitan coalition assembled by Green parties and a coalition assembled by radical-right parties. To establish that this type of electoral competition reflects the emergence of a new social cleavage, we would need further evidence about its socioeconomic roots and partisan behavior; but our evidence suggests that the political coalitions assembled by radical-right and Green parties, often said to exemplify the two sides of this cleavage, are now more viable in electoral terms than the coalitions traditionally assembled by center-left and center-right parties.

Although our analysis is congruent in some respects with the probing analysis of electoral realignment by Kitschelt and Rehm (2022), it differs from theirs in some ways. In their formulations, partisan realignment is driven primarily by increases in the proportion of the electorate with tertiary education and more diverse levels of income, as well as shifts in party strategy that take advantage of variation in the views of people at different levels of income and education. Based on recent data, Kitschelt and Rehm (2022) argue that people with different levels of income and education have stable preferences on economic and cultural issues.

However, our results suggest that over longer periods of time those preferences may be rather fluid. Although we group voters by occupation, rather than by income and education, and find some stability over time in the positions those occupational groups occupy relative to one another in the electoral space, we also observe substantial movements over time in their economic and cultural attitudes, including the emergence of gaps between them that can alter the viability of the coalitions assembled by various parties. We agree that realignment is taking place, as the prominence of cultural issues draws more highly educated voters toward the political left and those with less education to the political right (see also Gingrich and Häusermann 2015; Gethin et al. 2022). But our analysis suggests that the fate of specific political blocs, including on the left, may depend more heavily on shifts in issue salience and on changes in a relatively fluid set of voter preferences than some other approaches allow.

4.4 Robustness Tests

To assess the robustness of our conclusions, we also compare the viability of the four types of coalitions when the occupational groups composing them are allowed to vary, subject to some criteria that preserve the basic nature of the coalition. These criteria are: the center-right coalition must include managers or small employers; the center-left should include professionals or senior white-collar employees and either trades and crafts workers or production workers; and the radical-right coalition must include small employers and some segment of manual workers. The specifications for the cosmopolitan coalitions do not change. We then calculate the viability of coalitions (as in Table 3) for all possible occupational coalitions subject to these criteria at each of the three periods in time. Appendix G reports which of all these possible coalitions emerged as most viable in each period (column 2) and how viable they were under conditions that vary issue salience, as in Table 3. In many cases, the occupational groups in the coalition that emerges as most viable match our prior specifications. Regardless of their precise composition, the relative viability of the coalitions for different types of parties does not change much from the relative viability reported in Table 3; and, at each time period and under all conditions of salience, the partisan coalitions that emerge as most viable exactly match the patterns found in Table 3.

As an additional robustness test, we also examine the movement of occupational groups in each national electoral space and replicate this coalitional analysis for individual countries. As Appendix D indicates, there are some national variations but also substantial commonalities in how these occupational groups move over time in each country. In each of them, all occupational groups move in cosmopolitan directions on cultural issues over time. In most countries, these groups also move to the left on economic issues between 1990 and 2006 and then back toward the center by 2018. By then, a significant gap on cultural issues has also appeared in all countries between professional or skilled white-collar workers and manual workers.

Based on these movements, we assess the relative viability of coalitions at the national level in all twenty-four of the country waves, under scenarios that vary the salience of economic versus cultural issues as we have done for the pooled sample (see Appendix H for the results). Again, there are some national variations, but the results are broadly congruent with the conclusions we have reached. When economic issues dominate electoral contestation, the coalitions associated with mainstream center-left and center-right parties emerge as the most viable in fourteen of the national cases and the radical-right in none. By contrast, when cultural issues dominate, a radical-right coalition becomes the most viable in sixteen cases. When economic and cultural issues are equally salient, the coalition most likely to be viable is the cosmopolitan coalition (in eighteen cases), while each of the other three partisan coalitions emerges as most viable in three national cases. In the most realistic contemporary scenario, based on the position of occupational groups in 2018 with economic and cultural issues equally salient, the most viable electoral coalition is generally a cosmopolitan coalition.

4.5 Electoral Turnout and Secular Occupational Change

Although shifts in issue salience and changes in attitudes are the most important factors affecting the political potential of the electoral coalitions examined here, at least two other factors might also influence their relative viability. The first are variations in the rate of electoral turnout across occupational groups. It is well-known that people with higher levels of education and income are more likely to vote, and this is borne out by our data for 2006, the only wave for which we have good evidence about turnout. When asked whether they voted in the last national election, 80 percent of managers and 91 percent of professionals, but only 68 percent of production workers and 78 percent of crafts and trade workers, said they had. Hence, electoral coalitions that depend on manual workers for votes, such as those of the center-left and radical-right, face an electoral disadvantage vis-à-vis coalitions that draw larger numbers of supporters from occupational groups that vote at high rates, such as the cosmopolitan coalition.

Secular changes in the occupational structure may also alter the relative viability of various coalitions. In recent decades, for instance, the cosmopolitan coalition has benefited, not only from shifts in issue salience and attitudes, but also from economic developments that have increased the numbers of people working in services, who form the principal constituents of that coalition. Judging from the occupations represented in our pooled sample, the share of the workforce available to the cosmopolitan coalition rose from 47 percent to 67 percent between 1990 and 2018. Conversely, in most of the countries examined here, the long-term loss of manufacturing jobs may be limiting the electoral potential of center-left and radical-right coalitions, which draw heavily on shrinking numbers of workers in production and crafts and trades. We estimate, for instance, that the share of the workforce available to the radical-right coalition, as we construe it, shrank from about 50 percent in 1990 to 41 percent in 2018.

4.6 Cross-National Variation

The most striking features in our data are the parallel trends over time that we find in most, if not all, of the countries in this study. As we have noted, the salience of cultural issues relative to economic issues has increased in all of them; and the movements of occupational groups across the electoral space of each nation display the common trends we have highlighted (see Appendix D). In every country, the cultural attitudes of most occupational groups have become more cosmopolitan over the past three decades; most groups moved to the left on economic issues in the first half of the period and then back toward the center in the subsequent fifteen years; and there is considerable cross-national similarity, as well as stability, in where occupational groups are positioned vis-à-vis one another in this electoral space.

Although they may remain to be discovered, we do not find especially systematic variations across types of welfare regimes or political economies in the relative salience of issues or the types of electoral coalitions that emerge as most viable, even though some other analyses might expect that (cf. Beramendi et al. 2015; Manow et al. 2018). However, these national cases do display some distinctive features relevant to the prospects for coalition formation, with identifiable roots in the complexion of their political economies and national political histories.

There is some evidence here, for instance, that cross-national variation in the pace and direction of structural economic change, linked to differences in national political economies, is conditioning both the attitudes of citizens and the relative viability of various types of electoral coalitions. Employment in services (and in high-end services) has grown more substantially in Sweden, Norway, and the Netherlands than it has in many other countries. This shift in the occupational structure was initially inspired by the types of social democratic welfare states the Nordic nations developed, which expanded publicly provided social services (Esping-Andersen 1990). But the transition to services was then propelled forward by rapid transitions in these countries toward the economic endeavors of a knowledge economy, including growth in high-end business services (Wren 2013; Thelen 2014).

Since the interpersonal contact associated with positions in services and the levels of education demanded by jobs in the knowledge economy tend to promote cosmopolitan values, it is not surprising that the citizens in these three countries begin the period we examine with cultural views that are considerably more cosmopolitan than those held by citizens elsewhere; and the cultural views of Swedes and Norwegians move farther in cosmopolitan directions over these decades than cultural views do elsewhere. Although this type of occupational structure may improve the prospects for cosmopolitan coalitions in numerical terms, the relative viability of such a coalition depends more heavily on how various occupational groups are positioned vis-à-vis one another in the electoral space. In the Netherlands, for instance, this has rendered a cosmopolitan coalition especially viable, whereas the radical-right coalition emerges as most viable in Norway in 2018.

In Italy and the United States, by contrast, the prospects for radical-right coalitions may be somewhat better than they are elsewhere because small employers, who are a key component of those coalitions, compose an especially large share of their labor force. At about 11 percent in our data, that share is twice as large as it is in most of the other countries we consider (see also Beramendi et al. 2015). The occupational groups of these two countries also retain more traditional cultural views than they do elsewhere, presumably because these are the only two countries in our sample in which religious attendance remains high. And Americans' views on economic issues also tend to remain more conservative throughout the period than they do elsewhere, as might be expected given the long-standing stance of American governments regarding state intervention (Pontusson 2005; Hacker and Pierson 2016). These factors contribute to the fact that the United States is the only country in which a center-right coalition emerges as especially viable in 2018.

Multiple features of a country's political history can influence the positions of occupational groups in the electoral space, and hence the viability of various coalitions. In France and Italy, for instance, two countries with histories of political radicalism, fueled in the early postwar years by powerful Communist parties and perpetuated by politically oriented trade union movements, divisions between occupational groups on economic issues were especially pronounced in 1990 and 2006. In France, the economic views of small employers also tend to be farther left than they are elsewhere – perhaps the legacy of a republican tradition of protest in which small employers have been active participants (Berger 1977). By contrast, the economic and cultural views of occupational groups in Germany converged more sharply between 1990 and 2006 than they did in most other countries – likely the reflection of a unification process that saw the Eastern Länder integrated with those in the West during those years – making coalition formation considerably easier in Germany in 2018 than it was in 1990 (See Appendix D).

In this context, it is worth underlining that, although cultural issues have become increasingly important to electoral competition in recent decades, voters' views on economic issues remain consequential for the formation of electoral coalitions and corresponding partisan success. The prospects for a cosmopolitan coalition in the Netherlands were especially auspicious in 2018, for instance, because the economic as well as the cultural views of the three groups of service-sector workers composing it were very similar. Conversely, radical-right coalitions were more viable in Norway, France, and the United States than in many other nations in 2018 because manual workers held views on economic issues that were especially close to those of small employers.

National variations in voter turnout can also affect the viability of rival coalitions, and turnout among the working class depends to some extent on how it is organized in each political economy. According to our 2006 data, voter turnout among white-collar workers did not differ much across countries, but it was much more varied among production workers. Although turnout among production workers generally ran between 60 and 70 percent, it was closer to 70 percent of those workers in France, Italy, Norway, and Sweden, where trade unions are typically engaged with political issues, and only about 60 percent in Britain, the United States, and Germany, where trade unions are weaker or less involved in politics. As a result, radical-right or center-left coalitions that depend on support from production workers may have advantages in the Nordic nations, as well as France and Italy, that they do not enjoy elsewhere. Whether the center-left or radical-right will benefit depends, of course, on how strongly these trade unions agitate in favor of specific parties. Compared to nonmembers, trade union members are generally more likely to vote for social democratic parties and somewhat less likely to vote for radical-right parties, but these effects are often small and vary across countries (Rydgren 2009; Mosimann et al. 2019).

In sum, our analysis suggests that the viability of alternative coalitions is very sensitive to the positions that occupational groups take up within the electoral space; and, while those positions are affected by a nation's political economy, they can also be conditioned by many features of national political histories that defy standard typologies.

5 Conclusion

Using measures comparable across countries and time, we have examined the movement of occupational groups within the electoral space over the past thirty years in eight developed democracies with a view to assessing some prominent contentions about how electoral competition has changed and why mainstream parties are losing support to challenger parties. Combining this data with evidence for the movement of political parties and changes in the salience of economic and cultural issues, we find support for some of the most important of those contentions. We then applied spatial analysis to this data to assess the relative viability of the electoral coalitions typically formed by mainstream and challenger parties. The results augment a literature that has been based largely on cross-sectional analyses or on electoral developments considered over shorter periods of time.

We find that differences in the views of people in these occupational groups on economic issues declined modestly over those decades – albeit more modestly in some countries and more dramatically in others. Perhaps our most striking finding is that the attitudes of all occupational groups to cultural issues have become steadily more cosmopolitan over time. That point is worth under-lining at a moment when so much attention is being devoted to populist politicians who defend traditional values. But differences of opinion on cultural issues have been increasing, especially between blue-collar and white-collar workers. The views of many Western electorates are significantly more frag-mented on cultural issues than they were in 1990. As a result, challenger parties have new opportunities for rallying support, and mainstream parties have found it more difficult to hold their electoral coalitions together.

We also find that the political salience of cultural issues has been rising relative to the salience of economic issues. The principal axis of electoral competition has shifted toward the vertical, as partisan competition over eco-nomic issues has become less intense and conflict over cultural issues more central to electoral rivalry. Our evidence indicates that the electoral coalitions typically assembled by mainstream center-left and center-right parties tend to be more viable when economic issues are more salient than cultural issues. Hence, these shifts in salience have disadvantaged mainstream parties and rendered the electoral coalitions formed by radical-right and Green parties more viable over time. That helps to explain why radical-right and Green parties have become important contenders for political power. They now anchor the principal axis of political competition, which runs along a diagonal in this two-dimensional electoral space.

These developments presage a highly conflictual electoral politics. Since it is often easier for political parties to compromise on economic issues than on cultural ones, the increasing salience of cultural issues has rendered politics uglier in many nations. We find that the parties benefiting the most from the salience of cultural issues are radical-right parties; and their rise has inspired higher levels of affective polarization – leading citizens to vote against other parties rather than for their own, on emotional as much as utilitarian grounds, and to see politics in Manichean terms that have led some to question the legitimacy of election results (Gidron et al. 2020; Harteveld et al. 2022).

Our analysis suggests that the capacity of mainstream center-left and center-right parties to counteract these trends and hold onto governing positions without help from other parties is limited. Deep divisions on cultural issues have driven a stake through the electoral coalitions on which those parties once depended. As white-collar workers embrace more cosmopolitan cultural stances and blue-collar workers cling to more traditional views, it is no longer enough for those parties to find common ground among occupational groups on economic issues.

Although considerable attention has been devoted to the dilemmas these developments pose for center-left parties, those dilemmas are equally acute for mainstream center-right parties (Gidron 2020; Bale and Kaltwasser 2021). In the context that most closely resembles electoral politics today, when occupational groups are positioned in the electoral space as they were in 2018 and cultural and economic issues are equally salient to partisan competition, the evidence presented in Table 3 and Appendix H suggests that center-right parties will find it is even more difficult than center-left parties to form viable electoral coalitions without making pacts with radical right parties.

For readers who favor center-left economic policies and cosmopolitan values, the one piece of good news in our results is that there seems to be considerable potential in what we have described as a "cosmopolitan coalition" assembled from white-collar workers and others working in a variety of service positions. When economic and cultural issues are equally salient to electoral competition, this coalition emerges as the most viable, because most workers in services have relatively cosmopolitan values and the views of people in professional and white-collar occupations have moved to the left on economic issues, bringing them closer to the views of lower-level service workers. In some cases, center-left parties may be able to secure office on the back of such a coalition, although, in countries with electoral systems based on proportional representation this is more likely to be the basis for governing coalitions formed between Green parties, which attract sociocultural professionals, and social democratic parties, which may have more appeal for lower-level service workers. Some analysts argue that the future of the political left in Europe lies in such coalitions (Häusermann and Kitschelt 2023).

It is worth asking how the increasing salience of environmental issues might affect these trends. In the context of a climate crisis, environmental issues are becoming more relevant to voting behavior in all the countries we examine, but they do not figure in our analysis because we do not have comparable measures for people's views about them over a long period of time. Hence, what we can say about them must be somewhat speculative. Environmental issues have both economic and cultural dimensions. Efforts to reduce pollution or to shift energy sources to slow the rate of climate change engage economic interests. They impose costs on workers in some industries and offer benefits to employees in some competing sectors. But saving the environment is an endeavor with collective benefits that many people, especially in younger generations, have embraced on behalf of humanity as a cultural ideal (Inglehart 1977; Talshir 2002).

In keeping with this idealism, in the developed democracies the people most concerned about environmental issues tend to have relatively cosmopolitan views on other cultural issues (Dolezal 2010; Rohrschneider et al. 2014). In line with that, support for environmental protection has been especially strong among sociocultural professionals and people with a tertiary education (Poguntke 1987). One implication is that, as the electoral salience of environmental issues increases, the salience of cultural issues to politics is unlikely to decline. Indeed, Green parties combine strong support for environmental protection with support for other types of cosmopolitan values (van Haute 2016).

However, since people's attitudes toward environmental issues can also be driven by economic interests, there is some potential for conflict, notably between white-collar workers, who tend to favor environmental protection, and blue-collar workers whose livelihoods might be threatened by some types of environmental initiatives (Dolezal 2010; Otjes and Krouwel 2022). Where that conflict materializes, it could exacerbate the division already apparent between those two groups on cultural issues. Thus, as the climate crisis deepens, we can expect support for environmental protection to rise, but environmental issues may not provide a solid basis for a new solidarity across occupational groups, except in localized contexts where everyone suffers from environmental degradation. In sum, the rising salience of environmental issues may increase support for Green parties, rendering them more important partners in governing coalitions, but it is unlikely to provide the basis for a new coalition transcending the divisions we have found between blue-collar and white-collar workers.

It is important to note, however, that the electoral developments we have identified are not necessarily inexorable trends. The portrait of the electoral space that emerges from our evidence is one of flux rather than stability. Some of the movements of occupational groups within this electoral space between 1990 and 2006, for instance, were quite different from those that took place between 2006 and 2018. The earlier period saw most groups move to the left on economic issues and assume more similar positions on cultural issues, while the later one saw some occupational groups move back toward the right on economic issues, while new divisions emerged over cultural issues. Although intense partisan conflict over cultural issues may continue, there are also good reasons for expecting the salience of economic issues to rise again in the wake of inflation, an energy crisis, and recessions in some countries, much as it did after previous recessions. If economic issues do become increasingly salient, the relative viability of electoral coalitions could shift once again and we might see growing support for more interventionist economic policies in the coming years (see also Hall 2022a).

Several caveats must accompany this analysis. Given the extent to which people's jobs condition their economic and cultural attitudes (Kitschelt and Rehm 2014), we think that occupational coalitions command attention.

However, occupational groups are not the only social groups from which coalitions can be formed (cf. Liberini et al. 2020) and, as we have noted, parties can mount appeals that do not turn on the political preferences of social groups over economic and cultural issues (cf. Healy and Malhotra 2013; Green and Jennings 2017). We have emphasized developments on the "demand side" of politics but the outcomes of elections also turn, of course, on developments on its "supply side" that we have not considered, such as the types of parties contending for votes and the strategies they adopt to fend off their competitors (Meguid 2005).

It may also be possible to form occupational coalitions based on preferences that are more specific than those tapped by our measures for economic and cultural attitudes. A recent literature suggests, for example, that various occupational groups support different types of social policies (Abou-Chadi and Wagner 2019; Green-Pedersen and Jensen 2019; Häusermann et al. 2022). However, it is not yet clear that preferences over types of social policies affect voting decisions substantially more than the broad economic and cultural attitudes on which we concentrate, especially since party manifestos continue to highlight the issues tapped by our measures (cf. Garritzmann et al. 2018). We also lack data on some intermediate occupational categories, such as higher-level technical workers, from which more fine-grained coalitions might be formed. Since technically oriented professionals tend to have economic views to the right of sociocultural professionals (Oesch 2013b; Wren and Rehm 2013), some center-right electoral coalitions may be more viable than our calculations suggest.

However, this analysis opens promising agendas for further research. Although we believe that the national nature of electoral campaigns makes it reasonable to treat the salience of economic and cultural issues as general features of the electoral context, some occupational groups may give more weight in their voting decisions to economic issues, and others to cultural issues (Lachat 2008; Lefkofridi et al. 2014). The estimations reported in Table 2 indicate, for example, that in 2018 the political engagement of professionals and workers in crafts and trades may have been inspired by economic issues, while skilled white-collar workers seemed to care more about cultural issues. But these are relatively crude estimates for the relative importance that voters attach to economic and cultural issues, and there is scope for more research into such questions. Similarly, although we have made some observations about how variations in turnout affect the viability of coalitions, we see promise in further research into these matters.

Many studies of political behavior focus on short-term electoral changes. By charting the movement of occupational groups within the electoral space over thirty years, this study directs attention toward the importance of considering longer-term changes in electoral behavior and what drives them – essentially "big, slow-moving processes" of the sort that Pierson (2003) identified. We lay the groundwork for asking: How should long-term movements in the positions of occupational groups be explained? Is the growing cosmopolitanism of the electorate largely a matter of generational replacement or changes in the composition of employment? Why do the economic views of most groups shift to the left between 1990 and 2006 only to move to the right in subsequent decades? Why do professionals and skilled white-collar workers continue to take relatively left-wing positions on economic issues? How should cross-national variation in these long-term movements be explained?

We do not attempt dispositive answers to such questions, and they merit more attention. Further cross-sectional evidence can be brought to bear on them, and some studies have begun to approach such issues with data that covers longer periods of time (Beramendi et al. 2015; Iversen and Soskice 2015; Abou-Chadi and Hix 2021; Gethin et al. 2022; Kitschelt and Rehm 2022). But further research is needed into long-term changes in electoral behavior, especially with a view to exploring the relationships between changes in attitudes and the secular trends that have been transforming contemporary political economies. In that respect, we hope this Element advances an agenda that integrates the study of electoral politics with issues in comparative political economy.

Appendices

Appendix A: Classifications of Occupations from Surveys

SES occupational group	All WVS waves	EVS 2017 wave
Production workers	Unskilled manual workers Semi-skilled manual workers Agricultural workers	ISCO 62–3, 81–3, 92–4, 96 Stationary plant and machine operators, assemblers, drivers and mobile plant operators, cleaners and helpers, agricultural, forestry and fishery laborers; laborers in mining, construction, manufacturing and transport, food preparation assistants, refuse workers and other elementary workers; market-oriented skilled forestry, fishery and hunting workers; subsistence farmers, fishers, hunters and gatherers.
Manual crafts and trades workers	Foreman and supervisor Skilled manual workers	ISCO 71–5 Building and related trades workers, metal machinery and related trades workers, handicraft and printing workers, electrical and electronic trades workers, food processing, woodworking, garment and other craft and related trades workers.
Low-skill service workers	Junior level non manual workers	ISCO 41–44, 51–54, 91, 95 General and keyboard clerks, customer services clerks, numerical and material recording clerks, other clerical support workers, personal services workers, sales workers, personal care workers, protective services workers, cleaners and helpers, street and related sales and services workers.
Skilled white-collar workers	Middle-level nonmanual office workers Supervisory nonmanual office workers	ISCO 31–35 Science and engineering associate professionals, health associate professionals, business and administration associate professionals, information and communication technicians.

(cont.)

SES occupational group	All WVS waves	EVS 2017 wave
Professionals	Professional workers	ISCO 21–26 Science and engineering professionals, health professionals; teaching professionals; business and administration professionals; information and communications technology professionals; legal, social, and cultural professionals
Managers	Employer/manager of establishment with 10 or more employed	ISCO 11–14 Chief executives, senior officials and legislators; administrators and commercial managers; production and specialized service managers; hospitality, retail, and other services managers.
Small employers	Employer/manager of establishment with less than 10 employed Farmer, has own farm	ISCO 61 Market-oriented skilled agricultural workers and respondents who indicate they are self-employed.

Note: Members of the armed forces and those classified as "other" were not included in the sample.

Table AA1 Average levels of education and income within occupational groups (pooled sample)

Occupation	1990		2006		2018	
	Education	Income	Education	Income	Education	Income
PW	15.89	3.61	17.56	4.11	16.95	4.11
CT	16.88	4.28	18.46	4.31	17.16	4.52
SW	17.23	4.38	18.93	4.74	18.83	4.55
SE	17.18	4.96	19.74	5.34	19.20	5.64
WC	20.32	5.63	21.73	5.56	20.44	5.80
P	21.69	6.04	24.07	6.24	24.42	6.55
M	19.63	7.21	21.64	6.76	21.90	6.93

Note: Education is average age of completing education. Income is average income decile. The composition of the occupational groups is as listed in Figure 2.

Appendix B: WVS/EVS Questions Used to Construct the Economic and Cultural Indices

Economic Index

E035: On this card you see a number of opposite views on various issues. How would you place your views on this scale? Incomes should be made more equal ... 1 2 3 4 5 6 7 8 9 10 ... There should be greater incentives for individual effort.

E036: Private ownership of business and industry should be increased ... 1 2 3 4 5 6 7 8 9 10 ... Government ownership of business and industry should be increased.

E037: Individuals should take more responsibility for providing for themselves ... 1 2 3 4 5 6 7 8 9 10 ... The state should take more responsibility to ensure that everyone is provided for.

E038: People who are unemployed should have to take any job available or lose their unemployment benefits ... 1 2 3 4 5 6 7 8 9 10 ... People who are unemployed should have the right to refuse a job they do not want.

E039: Competition is good. It stimulates people to work hard and develop new ideas ... 1 2 3 4 5 6 7 8 9 10 ... Competition is harmful, it brings out the worst in people.

Cultural Index

Please tell me for each of the following whether you think it can always be justified, never be justified, or something in between, using this card – never 1 2 3 4 5 6 7 8 9 10 always

F118: Abortion   F120: Homosexuality

Here are changes in our way of life that might take place in the near future. Please tell me for each one, if it were to happen whether you think it would be a good thing, a bad thing, or don't you mind?

E018: Greater respect for authority. 1 good, 2 bad, 3 don't mind

C001: When jobs are scarce, men have more right to a job than women. 1 agree, 2 disagree, 3 neither

On this list are various groups of people. Could you mention any that you would not like to have as neighbors? Mentioned: 1 Not mentioned: 2.

A124.02: People of a different race

A124.05: Muslims

A124.06: Immigrants/foreign workers

Appendix C: Locating Citizens in the Electoral Space

To locate voters in a two-dimensional space, we estimate a confirmatory model of multidimensional item response theory parameters (Chalmers 2012). Given the ordinal nature of the data, the model is based on Samejima's (1969) multidimensional ordinal response model yielding the factor loadings as below.

Table AC1 Factor loadings from item response model

Question	Factor 1	Factor 2
Income inequality	0.35	
Private ownership	−0.61	
Govt responsibility	−0.59	
Unemployment benefits	−0.47	
Competition good	−0.58	
Abortion		0.72
Homosexuality		0.85
Respect for authority		−0.27
Women right to work		−0.51
Neighbors – race		−0.53
Neighbors – Muslims		−0.40
Neighbors – immigrants		−0.42

Appendix D: The Location of Occupational Groups in the Electoral Space: 1990, 2006, and 2018

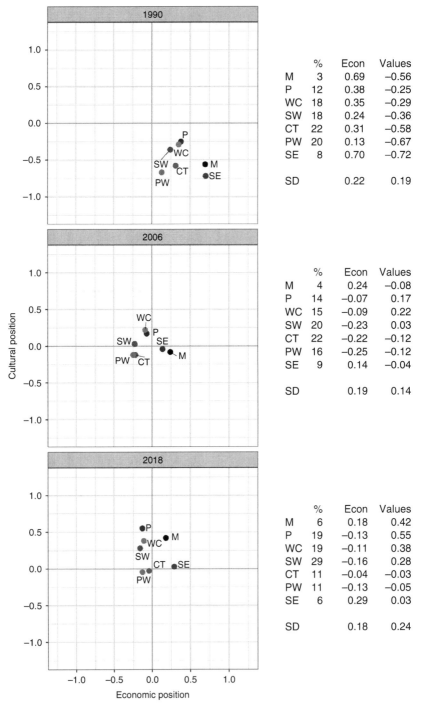

Figure AD1 All countries

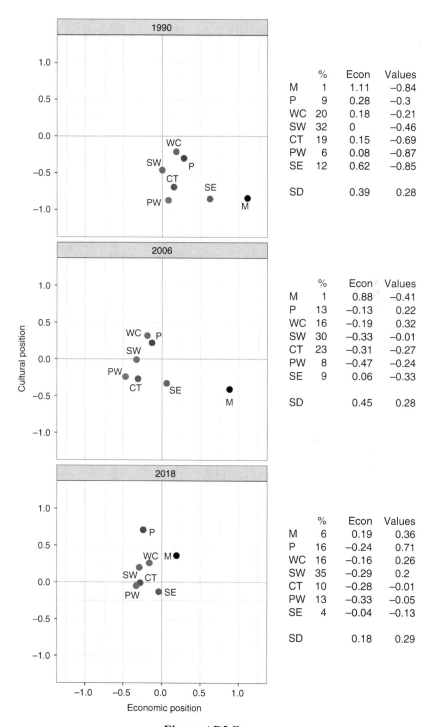

Figure AD2 France

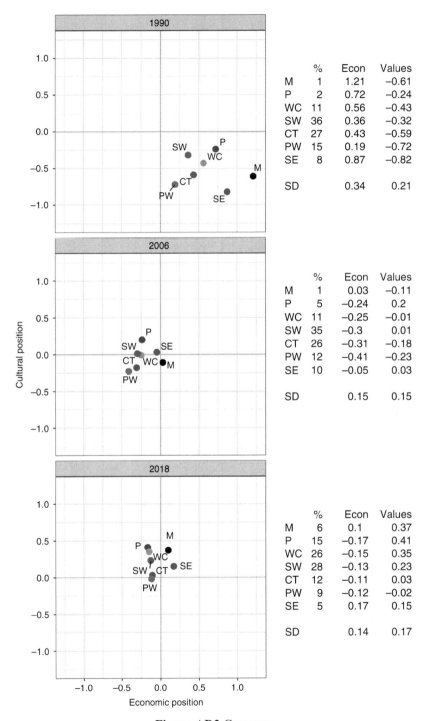

Figure AD3 Germany

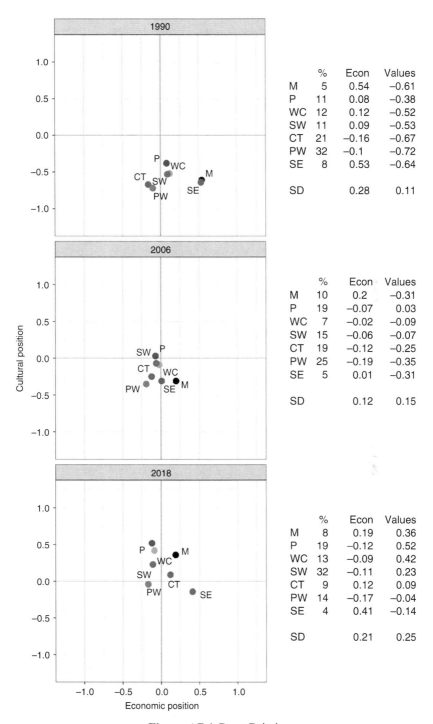

Figure AD4 Great Britain

Appendices

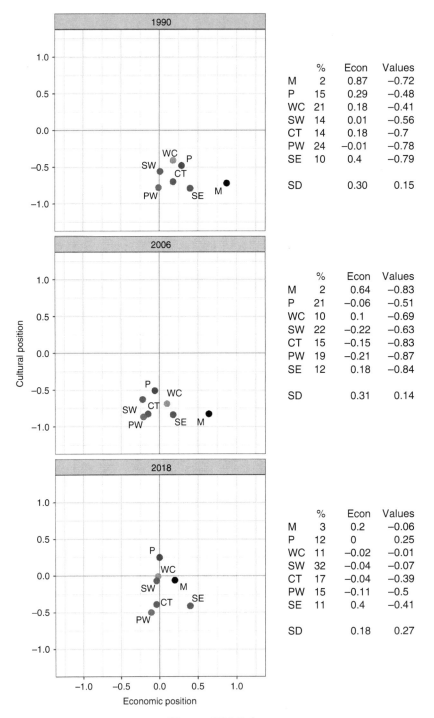

Figure AD5 Italy

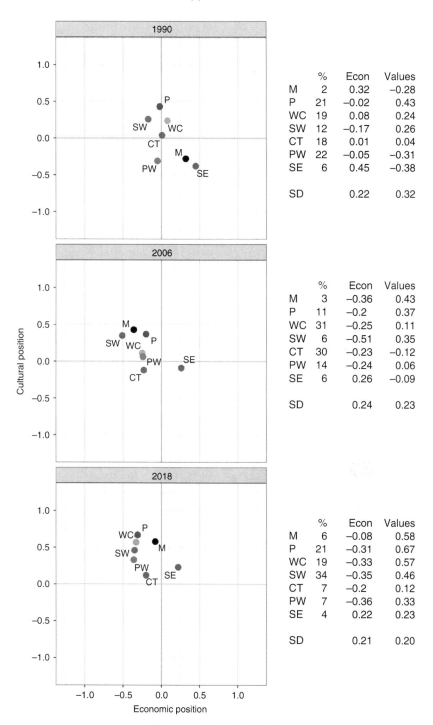

Figure AD6 Netherlands

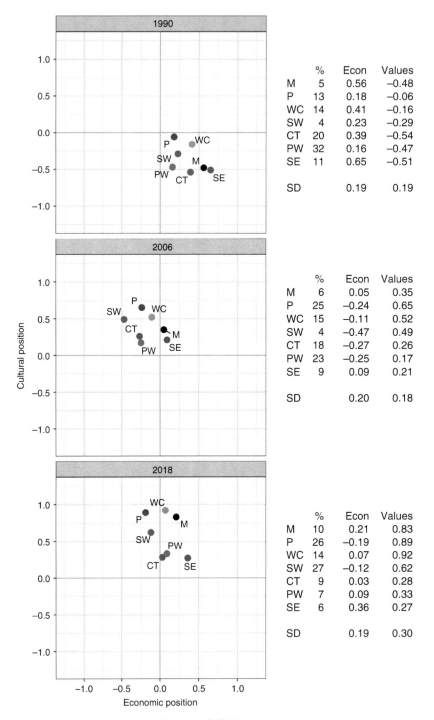

Figure AD7 Norway

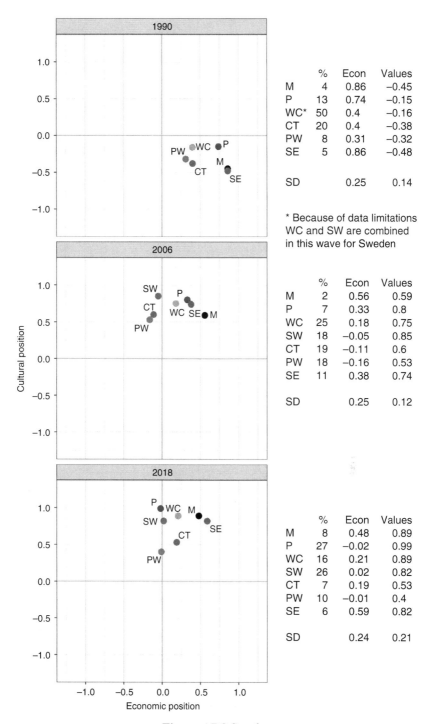

Figure AD8 Sweden

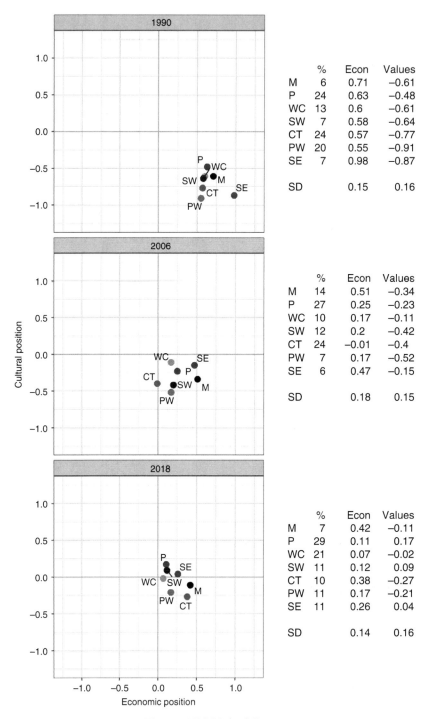

Figure AD9 United States

Note: M – managers; P – professionals; WC – skilled white-collar workers; SW – lower-level service workers; SE – small employers; CT – manual workers in crafts and trades; PW – manual production workers. SD is the standard deviation of views among occupational groups on each set of issues in that wave.

Source: Authors' calculations from WVS/EVS. % is national proportion of workforce from WVS samples.

Appendix E: Locating Parties in the Electoral Space

1. Comparative Manifesto Project items used for locating parties in the electoral space

Economic left:

- 409: Keynesian demand management
- 413: Nationalization
- 504: Welfare state expansion
- 701: Labor groups: positive

Economic right:

- 401: Free market economy
- 403: Market regulation
- 505: Welfare state limitation
- 702: Labor groups: negative

Values left:

- 602: National way of life: negative (opposition to nationalism)
- 604: Traditional morality (negative)
- 607: Multiculturalism: positive
- 705: Underprivileged minority groups (gay/immigrant/indigenous etc.)

Values right:

- 601: National way of life: negative (appeals to nationalism)
- 603: Traditional morality (positive)
- 608: Multiculturalism (negative).

2. Procedure used for aggregating these variables into scales (following Lowe et al. 2011):

$$\text{econ.position} = \log\left[\frac{\text{econ.right} + 0.5}{\text{econ.left} + 0.5}\right]$$

$$\text{values.position} = \log\left[\frac{\text{values.left} + 0.5}{\text{values.right} + 0.5}\right]$$

Appendix F: Issue Salience

The salience of a type of issue in party platforms is based on the share of sentences or "quasi-sentences" that refer to the following categories grouped under "cultural" or "economic" issues, and the overall measure for issue salience in each country is the average share of quasi-sentences pertinent to each category in party manifestos weighted by the party's share of the vote. The cross-national indicators in Figure 7 are an average of these country-specific values.

Variables included in cultural category:

501: Environmental protection
502: Culture (state funding for arts and sport)
503: Equality ("concept of social justice and need for fair treatment of all")
601: National way of life ("general" and immigration [negative])
602: National way of life ("general II" and immigration [positive])
603: Traditional morality
604: Traditional morality (negative)
605: Law and order
606: Law and order (negative)
607: Multiculturalism
608: Multiculturalism (negative)

Variables included in economic category:

401: Free market economy
402: Incentives
403: Market regulation
404: Economic planning
405: Corporatism/mixed economy
406: Protectionism
407: Protectionism (negative)
408: Economic goals
409: Keynesian demand management
410: Economic growth
411: Technology and Infrastructure
412: Controlled economy
413: Nationalization
414: Economic orthodoxy
415: Marxist analysis
504: Welfare state expansion
505: Welfare state limitation

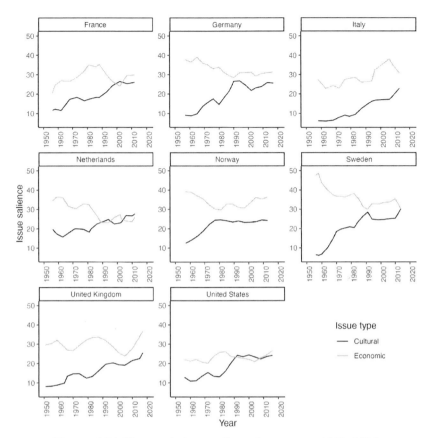

Figure AF1 Changes in issue salience by country, 1950–2020

Table AF1 The relationship between views on economic and cultural issues and votes for party families in 1990 and 2018 within the full sample

	Dependent variable:				
	Center-left	Center-right	Radical-left	Radical-right	Green
	(1)	(2)	(3)	(4)	(5)
Economic x 1990	−0.377***	0.394***	−0.486***	0.348***	−0.258***
	(0.0263)	(0.026)	(0.053)	(0.072)	(0.052)
Economic x 2018	−0.358***	0.587***	− 0.739***	0.235***'	−0.282***
	(0.024)	(0.023)	(0.034)	(0.035)	(0.041)
Cultural x 1990	0.175***	−0.478***	0.413***	−0.263***	0.759***
	(0.1032)	(0.033)	(0.059)	(0.037)	(0.065)
Cultural x 2018	0.070***	− 0.302***	0.149***	−0.263***	0.381***
	(0.025)	(0.023)	(0.034)	(0.037)	(0.046)
Education (years)	−0.14***	−0.005	0.008**	−0.027***	0.026
	(0.003)	(0.003)	(0.004)	(0.005)	(0.005)
Income	−0.052***	0.075***	−0.039***	−0.044***	−0.011
	(0.006)	(0.006)	(0.010)	(0.012)	(0.011)
Sex (male)	−0.004	0.010***	0.0041	−1.050***	0.115
	(0.032)	(0.031)	(0.049)	(0.060)	(0.060)
Age	−0.0004	0.010***	0.001	−0.008***	−0.021***
	(0.001)	(0.001)	(0.001)	(0.002)	(0.002)
Country (Germany)	0.025	0.252***	0.030	−1.050***	0.115
	(0.056)	(0.057)	(0.080)	(0.133)	(0.084)
Country (Great Britain)	0.449***	0.339***	−3.124***	−0.620***	−0.613***
	(0.067)	(0.065)	(0.089)	(0.102)	(0.113)
Country (Norway)	0.139**	0.085	−0.075	0.894***	−2.233***
	(0.065)	(0.068)	(0.092)	(0.099)	(0.186)
Country (Sweden)	0.454***	0.158**	−0.624***	−0.427***	−0.730***
	(0.074)	(0.077)	(0.114)	(0.144)	(0.119)
Country (United States)	0.998***	0.140*	–	–	–
	(0.080)	(0.081)	–	–	–
Wave (2017)	−0.755***	0.042	0.406***	1.120***	0.062
	(0.041)	(0.041)	(0.067)	(0.098)	(0.082)
Constant	0.156*	−1.671***	−2.687***	−2.455***	−1.657***
	(0.094)	(0.095)	(0.134)	(0.182)	(0.151)
Observations	21,505	21,505	18,267	17,675	17,896

Note: *p<0.1; **p<0.05; ***p<0.01

Appendix G: Coalition Potential in 1990, 2006, and 2018 with Variable Coalitions

Coalition	Composition	Workforce share	Max distance economic axis	Max distance cultural axis	Triangle size
1990					
Center-left	WC + CT + SW	57%	**11**	29	38
Center-right	M + CT + SE	33%	39	16	56
Cosmopolitan	P + WC + SW	47%	14	**11**	**21**
Radical-right	CT + M + SE	33%	39	16	56
2006					
Center-left	P + SW + CT	56%	**16**	29	39
Center-right	P + WC + SE	38%	23	26	43
Cosmopolitan	P + WC + SW	49%	**16**	19	**31**
Radical-right	CT + PW + SE	47%	39	**8**	51
2018					
Center-left	WC + CT+ SW	58%	12	41	51
Center-right	M + WC + LS	54%	34	14	45
Cosmopolitan	P + WC +SW	66%	**5**	27	**31**
Radical-right*	CT + PW + SE	41%	42	**8**	51

Note: This table reports the coalitions with any composition appropriate to their labels that minimize the distance from the relevant centroid to their vertices. See Section 4.4 for the conditions circumscribing variation in these coalitions. The most viable coalitions are in **bold**. All distances multiplied by 100. Workforce share is based on the proportion of workers in each occupation in the weighted WVS sample. *Workforce share based on labor force surveys to correct for underrepresentation of some groups in the 2017 EVS. For the composition of the occupational groups see the note to Figure 2.

Appendix H: Coalition Potential in 1990, 2006, and 2018 by Country

Coalition	1990				2006					2018				
	Share	Max distance		Triangle	Share	Max distance		Triangle		Share	Max distance		Triangle	
		Econ	Cultural	Size		Econ	Cultural	Size	Change		Econ	Cultural	Size	Change
	%				%					%				
France														
Center-left	48	**13**	48	61	52	**18**	59	76	+15	42	12	72	81	+5
Center-right	42	44	64	95	38	25	65	70	-25	36	20	84	89	+19
Cosmopolitan	63	28	25	**45**	59	20	33	**46**	+1	66	**13**	51	67	+21
Radical-right	37	54	**18**	73	41	53	**9**	61	-12	28*	29	**12**	**39**	-22
Germany														
Center-left	41	**29**	35	47	42	7	38	41	-6	53	6	38	47	+6
Center-right	22	31	58	78	26	20	**21**	39	-39	46	34	26	54	+15
Cosmopolitan	49	36	**19**	**48**	51	**6**	**21**	**28**	-20	70	**4**	18	**20**	-8
Radical-right	51	68	23	83	48	36	26	52	-29	25	29	**17**	43	-9
Great Britain														
Center-left	44	28	29	49	44	10	28	34	-15	41	24	43	59	+25
Center-right	31	45	26	65	31	8	34	38	-27	36	53	66	107	+69
Cosmopolitan	34	**4**	15	**20**	41	**5**	12	**16**	+4	65	**3**	29	**33**	+17
Radical-right	60	69	**8**	89	49	20	**10**	27	-36	27	58	**23**	72	+45

Italy													
Center-left	51	**11**	29	**39**	46	25	32	48	+9	40	**4**	64	68	+20
Center-right	46	14	34	47	43	**24**	33	**44**	-3	33	42	66	93	+49
Cosmopolitan	50	22	38	52	52	32	18	**44**	-8	54	**4**	32	**39**	-5
Radical-right	48	41	**9**	47	46	39	**4**	48	+1	43	51	**11**	65	+17
Netherlands													
Center-left	58	**10**	39	45	71	**5**	49	**52**	+7	48	13	55	69	+17
Center-right	46	47	81	111	47	51	46	86	-25	45	55	44	90	+4
Cosmopolitan	52	25	**19**	**40**	48	31	26	54	+14	75	**4**	**21**	**22**	-32
Radical-right	46	50	42	85	49	50	**18**	71	-14	19	58	**21**	74	+3
Norway													
Center-left	47	**23**	48	66	58	**16**	39	51	-15	49	**26**	64	92	+41
Center-right	39	47	45	74	49	33	44	62	-12	46	55	65	107	+45
Cosmopolitan	32	**23**	23	**41**	44	36	16	**48**	+7	67	**26**	30	52	+4
Radical-right	63	49	**7**	53	50	36	**9**	**48**	-5	23	33	**6**	**41**	-7
Sweden**													
Center-left	83	**34**	23	**56**	51	44	20	54	-2	51	**23**	46	64	+10
Center-right	67	46	33	71	43	**20**	**6**	**25**	-46	50	61	**17**	68	+43
Cosmopolitan	63	**34**	**1**	—	50	38	10	44	—	69	**23**	**17**	**36**	-12
Radical-right	33	55	16	70	48	54	21	73	+3	23	60	42	82	+9

(cont.)

Coalition	1990				2006					2018				
	Share	Max distance		Triangle	Share	Max distance		Triangle		Share	Max distance		Triangle	
		Econ	Cultural	Size		Econ	Cultural	Size	Change		Econ	Cultural	Size	Change
United States														
Center-left	60	6	29	31	60	26	29	47	+16	60	31	44	64	+17
Center-right	44	38	39	67	44	30	**12**	39	-28	61	19	**19**	**34**	-5
Cosmopolitan	44	**5**	16	**20**	49	**8**	31	**36**	+16	62	**5**	**19**	**34**	-2
Radical-right	50	43	**14**	59	37	48	37	73	+14	32	21	31	47	-26

Notes: Most viable coalitions in **bold**. The "Change" columns indicate change in the size of the triangles as measured by the centroids since the previous period. The "Share" columns indicate the share of the workforce in the coalition from the WVS/EVS samples. *The size of the radical-right coalition in France in 2018 may be understated because the occupational groups included in it are underrepresented in the 2017–18 EVS survey. **Because of data limitations, figures for Sweden in 1990 use 'service workers' for SW (lower-level service workers) or WC (high-skill white-collar workers).

Tally of Winning Coalitions in All Country Cases by the Relative Salience of Economic and Cultural Issues

	Most successful coalition			
	Center-left	Center-right	Cosmopolitan	Radical-right
Most salient issue				
Economic	12	2	15	0
Cultural	0	5	7	16
Both	3	3	18	3

Note: Totals in rows vary because of ties in cases in which two equally successful coalitions are counted.

Appendix I: Differences in Average Attitudes by Sociodemographic Groups

		%	Economic attitudes			Cultural attitudes		
			1990	2006	2018	1990	2006	2018
Gender								
	Male	49%	0.38	−0.06	0.03	−0.53	−0.11	0.06
	Female	51%	0.23	−0.18	−0.13	−0.45	0.01	0.19
Age	**Over 65**	18%	0.43	−0.04	0.02	−0.96	−0.42	−0.2
	35–65	53%	0.34	−0.12	−0.04	−0.52	−0.01	0.18
	Under 35	29%	0.2	−0.17	−0.13	−0.23	0.09	0.29
Birth cohort								
	1920–39	21%	0.39	−0.03	0.05	−0.74	−0.43	−0.43
	1940–59	39%	0.3	−0.1	−0.02	−0.35	−0.08	0.04
	1960–79	40%	0.18	−0.15	−0.03	−0.23	0.06	0.21
Education								
	Low	68%	0.3	−0.15	−0.05	−0.58	−0.2	−0.01
	High	32%	0.34	−0.09	−0.08	−0.21	0.24	0.48
Income								
	Low	82%	0.3	−0.15	−0.09	−0.55	−0.07	0.09
	High	18%	0.37	0.06	0.08	−0.26	0.3	0.43

Notes: Higher scores indicate more conservative economic views and more cosmopolitan cultural views. High income indicates respondents in the top 30 percent and low income those in the bottom 70 percent of the income distribution. High education indicates people with a tertiary education (who left school at age 21 or above) and low education those without it. Cohorts are birth cohorts. Percent is proportion of the sample in each category averaged across all three waves.

References

Abou-Chadi, T. and Hix, S. (2021) Brahmin Left versus Merchant Right? Education, Class, Multiparty Competition and Redistribution in Western Europe. *British Journal of Sociology*, 72(1), 79–92.

Abou-Chadi, T. and Wagner, M. (2019) The Electoral Appeal of Party Strategies in Post-Industrial Democracies: When Can the Mainstream Left Succeed? *Journal of Politics*, 81, 1405–1419.

Abou-Chadi, T., Mitteregger, R., and Mudde, C. (2021) *Left Behind by the Working Class?* Berlin: Friedrich Ebert Stifgung.

Adams, J. F., Merrill, S., and Grofman, B. (2005) *A Unified Theory of Party Competition: A Cross-National Analysis Integrating Spatial and Behavioral Factors*. New York: Cambridge University Press.

Andersen, K. and Cook, E. A. (1985) Women, Work and Political Attitudes. *American Journal of Political Science*, 29(3), 606–625.

Ansell, B. and Gingrich, J. (2021) The End of Human Capital Solidarity? In F. M. Rosenbluth and M. Weir, eds., *Who Gets What? The New Politics of Insecurity*. New York: Cambridge University Press, pp. 52–78.

Ares, M. (2017) A New Working Class? A Cross-National and a Longitudinal Approach to Class Voting in Post-Industrial Societies. PhD thesis, European University Institute.

Ares, M. (2022) Issue Politicization and Social Class: How the Electoral Supply Activates Class Divides in Political Preferences. *European Journal of Political Research*, 61(2), 503–523.

Armingeon, K., Wenger, V., Wiedemeier, F., et al. (2019) Comparative Political Data Set 1960–2017. Institute of Political Science, University of Zurich.

Autor, D. and Dorn, D. (2013) The Growth of Low-Skill Service Jobs and the Polarization of the US Labor Market. *American Economic Review*, 103(5), 1553–1597.

Autor, D., Goldin, C., and Katz, L. F. (2020) Extending the Race between Education and Technology. *American Economic Association Papers and Proceedings*, 110 (May), 347–351.

Baccaro, L. and Howell, C. (2017) *Trajectories of Neoliberal Transformation*. New York: Cambridge University Press.

Baily, M. N. and Lawrence, R. Z. (2004) What Happened to the Great U.S. Jobs Machine? The Role of Trade and Electronic Offshoring. *Brookings Papers on Economic Activity*, 35(2), 211–284.

Bale, T. and Kaltwasser, C. R. (2021) *Riding the Populist Wave: Europe's Mainstream Right in Crisis.* Cambridge: Cambridge University Press.

Banaszak, L. A. and Plutzer, E. (1993) Contextual Determinants of Feminist Attitudes: National and Subnational Influences in Western Europe. *American Political Science Review*, 87(1), 145–157.

Banting, K. and Kymlicka, W. (2013) Is There Really a Retreat from Multiculturalism Policies? New Evidence from the Multiculturalism Policy Index. *Comparative European Politics*, 11(5), 577–598.

Beramendi, P., Häusermann, S., Kitschelt, H., and Kries, H.-P., eds. (2015) *The Politics of Advanced Capitalism.* New York: Cambridge University Press.

Berger, S. (1977) D'une boutique à l'autre: Changes in the Organization of the Traditional Middle Classes from the Fourth to Fifth Republics. *Comparative Politics*, 10(1), 121–136.

Berger, S. (2017) Populism and the Failures of Representation. *French Politics, Culture & Society*, 35(2), 21–31.

Berman, S. and Snegovaya, M. (2019) Populism and the Decline of Social Democracy. *Journal of Democracy*, 30(3), 5–19.

Bolzendahl, C. I. and Myers, D. J. (2004) Feminist Attitudes and Support for Gender Equality: Opinion Change in Women and Men, 1974–1998. *Social Forces*, 83(2), 759–790.

Bornschier, S. (2010) *Cleavage Politics and the Populist Right: The New Cultural Conflict in Western Europe.* Philadelphia, PA: Temple University Press.

Bornschier, S. and Kriesi, H.-P. (2013) The Populist Right, the Working Class and the Changing Face of Class Politics. In J. Rydgren, ed., *Class Politics and the Radical Right*, Abingdon: Routledge, pp. 10–30.

Bornschier, S., Häusermann, S., Zollinger, D., and Colombo, C. (2021) How "Us" and "Them" Relates to Voting Behavior – Social Structure, Social Identities and Electoral Choice. *Comparative Political Studies*, 54(20), 2087–2122.

Bromley, P. (2009) Cosmopolitanism in Civic Education: Exploring Cross-National Trends, 1970–2008. *Current Issues in Comparative Education*, 12(1), 33–44.

Burgoon, B. and Dekker, F. (2010) Flexible Employment, Economic Insecurity and Social Policy Preferences in Europe. *Journal of European Social Policy*, 20(2), 126–141.

Caramani, D. (2009) *The Nationalization of Politics: The Formation of National Electorates and Party Systems in Western Europe.* Cambridge: Cambridge University Press.

Caughey, D., O'Grady, T., and Warshaw, T. (2019) Policy Ideology in European Mass Publics 1981–2016. *American Political Science Review*, 113, 674–693.

Centeno M. A. and Cohen J. N. (2012) The Arc of Neoliberalism. *Annual Review of Sociology*, 38, 317–340.

Chalmers, R. P. (2012) Mirt: A Multidimensional Item Response Theory Package for the R Environment. *Journal of Statistical Software*, 48(6), 1–29.

Dalton, R. J. and Kuechler, M., eds. (1990) *Challenging the Political Order: New Social and Political Movements in Western Democracies*. New York: Oxford University Press.

Danieli, O., Gidron, N., Kikuchi, S., and Levy, R. (2022) Decomposing the Rise of the Populist Radical Right. SSRN 4255937. http://dx.doi.org/10.2139/ssrn.4255937.

De Vries, C. E., Hakhverdian, A., and Lancee, B. (2013) The Dynamics of Voters' Left/Right Identification: The Role of Economic and Cultural Attitudes. *Political Science Research and Methods*, 1(2), 223–238.

Dennison, J. (2019) A Review of Public Issue Salience: Determinants and Effects on Voting. *Political Studies Review*, 17(4), 436–446.

Dolezal, M. (2010) Exploring the Stabilization of a Political Force: The Social and Attitudinal Basis of Green Parties in the Age of Globalization. *West European Politics*, 33(3), 534–552.

Dolvik, J. E. and Martin, A., eds. (2015) *European Social Models from Crisis to Crisis*. Oxford: Oxford University Press.

Emmenger, P., Häusermann, S., Palier B., and Seeleib-Kaiser, M., eds. (2012) *The Age of Dualization: The Changing Face of Inequality in Deindustrializing Societies*. Oxford: Oxford University Press.

Eribon, D. (2013) *Returning to Reims*. Cambridge, MA: MIT Press.

Esping-Andersen, G. (1990) *Three Worlds of Welfare Capitalism*. Princeton, NJ: Princeton University Press.

Evans, G., ed. (1999) *The End of Class Politics?* Oxford: Oxford University Press.

Evans, G. and Hall, P. A. (2019) Representation Gaps: Changes in Popular Preferences and Party Positions over the Long Term in Developed Democracies. Paper presented at the Annual Meeting of the American Political Science Association, Washington, DC.

Evans, G. and Tilley, J. (2011) How Parties Shape Class Politics: Explaining the Decline of the Class Basis of Party Support. *British Journal of Political Science*, 42, 137–161.

Evans, G. and Tilley, J. (2017) *The New Politics of Class*. Oxford: Oxford University Press.

Fill, A. (2019) *The Political Economy of De-Liberalization*. Cham: Springer.

Garritzmann, J. L., Busemeyer, M. R., and Neimanns, E. (2018) Public Demand for Social Investment: New Supporting Coalitions for Welfare State Reform in Europe. *Journal of European Public Policy*, 25, 844–861.

Geering, D. and Häusermann, S. (2013) Changing Party Electorates and Economic Realignment. Unpublished manuscript.

Gethin, A., Martínez-Toledano, C., and Piketty, T. (2022) Brahmin Left versus Merchant Right: Changing Political Cleavages in 21 Western Democracies, 1948–2020. *Quarterly Journal of Economics*, 137(1), 1–48.

Gidron, N. (2020) Many Ways to Be Right: Cross-Pressured Voters in Western Europe. *British Journal of Political Science*, 52(1), 146–161.

Gidron, N. and Hall, P. A. (2017) The Politics of Social Status: Economic and Cultural Roots of the Populist Right. *British Journal of Sociology*, 68(S1), S57–S84.

Gidron, N. and Hall, P. A. (2019) Populism as a Problem of Social Integration. *Comparative Political Studies*, 53, 1027–1059.

Gidron, N. and Ziblatt, D. (2019) Center-Right Parties in Advanced Democracies. *Annual Review of Political Science*, 22, 17–35.

Gidron, N., Adams, J., and Horne, W. (2020) *American Affective Polarization in Comparative Perspective*. Cambridge: Cambridge University Press.

Gingrich, J. (2017) A New Progressive Coalition? The European Left in a Time of Change. *Political Quarterly*, 88, 39–51.

Gingrich, J. and Häusermann, S. (2015) The Decline of the Working-Class Vote, the Reconfiguration of the Welfare Support Coalition and Consequences for the Welfare State. *Journal of European Social Policy*, 25, 50–75.

Glyn, A. (2006) *Capitalism Unleashed*. Oxford: Oxford University Press.

Goos, M., Manning, A., and Salomons, A. (2009) Job Polarization in Europe. *American Economic Review*, 99, 58–63.

Goren, P. (2013) *On Voter Competence*. Oxford: Oxford University Press.

Grant, Z. P. and Tilley, J. (2022) Why the Left Has More to Lose from Ideological Convergence than the Right. *Party Politics* (OnlineFirst). https://doi.org/10.1177/13540688221097809.

Green, J. and Jennings, W. (2017) *The Politics of Competence: Parties, Public Opinion and Voters*. Cambridge: Cambridge University Press.

Green-Pedersen, C. and Jensen, C. (2019) Electoral Competition and the Welfare State. *West European Politics*, 42, 803–823.

Grzymala-Busse, A. (2019) The Failure of Europe's Mainstream Parties. *Journal of Democracy* 30(4), 35–47.

Hacker, J. S. and Pierson, P. (2016) *American Amnesia*. New York: Simon and Schuster.

Hall, P. A. (2022a) The Shifting Relationship between Postwar Capitalism and Democracy. *Government & Opposition*, 57(1), 1–30.

Hall, P. A. (2022b) Growth Regimes. *Business History Review*, 1–25. https://doi.org/10.1017/S0007680522000034.

Harteveld, E. (2016) Winning the Losers but Losing the Winners? The Electoral Consequences of the Radical Right Moving to the Economic Left. *Electoral Studies*, 44, 225–234.

Harteveld, E., Mendoza, P., and Rooduijn, M. (2022) Affective Polarization and the Populist Radical Right: Creating the Hating? *Government and Opposition*, 37, 703–727.

Häusermann, S. (2018) Social Democracy and the Welfare State in Context: The Conditioning Effect of Institutional and Party Competition. In P. Manow, B. Palier, and H. Schwander, eds., *Welfare Democracies and Party Politics*. Oxford: Oxford University Press, pp. 150–170.

Häusermann, S. and Kitschelt, H. (2023) *Beyond Social Democracy: Transformation of the Left in Emerging Knowledge Societies*. Cambridge: Cambridge University Press.

Häusermann, S. and Kriesi, H.-P. (2015) What Do Voters Want? Dimensions and Configurations in Individual Level Preferences and Party Choice. In P. Beramendi, S. Häusermann, H. Kitschelt, and H. Kriesi, eds., *The Politics of Advanced Capitalism*. New York: Cambridge University Press, pp. 202–230.

Häusermann, S., Kurer, T., and Schwander, H. (2015) High-Skilled Outsiders? Labor Market Vulnerability, Education and Welfare State Preferences. *Socio-Economic Review*, 13(2), 235–258.

Häusermann, S., Pinggera, M., Ares, M., and Enggist, M. (2022) Class and Social Policy in the Knowledge Economy. *European Journal of Political Research*, 61, 462–484.

Healy, A. and Malhotra, N. (2013) Retrospective Voting Reconsidered. *Annual Review of Political Science*, 16, 285–306.

Hillen, S. and Steiner, N. D. (2020) The Consequences of Supply Gaps in Two-Dimensional Policy Spaces for Voter Turnout and Political Support: The Case of Economically Left-Wing and Culturally Right-Wing Citizens in Western Europe. *European Journal of Political Research*, 59(2), 331–353.

Hobolt, S. B. and De Vries, C. E. (2020) *Political Entrepreneurs: The Rise of Challenger Parties in Europe*. Princeton, NJ: Princeton University Press.

Hochschild, A. R. (2016) *Strangers in Their Own Land*. New York: New Press.

Hooghe, L. and Marks, G. (2018) Cleavage Theory Meets Europe's Crises: Lipset, Rokkan and the Transnational Cleavage. *Journal of European Public Policy*, 25, 109–135.

Hopkin, J. (2020) *Anti-System Politics: The Crisis of Market Liberalism in Rich Democracies*. Oxford: Oxford University Press.

Hopkin, J. and Blyth, M. (2019) The Global Economics of European Populism: Growth Regimes and Party System Change in Europe. *Government and Opposition*, 54, 193–225.

Hopkins, D. J. (2018) *The Increasingly United States: How and Why American Political Behavior Nationalized*. Chicago, IL: University of Chicago Press.

Inglehart, R. F. (1977) *The Silent Revolution: Changing Values and Political Styles among Western Publics*. Princeton, NJ: Princeton University Press.

Inglehart, R. F. (1990) *Culture Shift in Advanced Industrial Societies*. Princeton, NJ: Princeton University Press.

Inglehart, R. F. (1997) *Modernization and Postmodernization: Cultural, Economic and Political Change in 43 Societies*. Princeton, NJ: Princeton University Press.

Ivarsflaten, E. (2005) The Vulnerable Populist Right Parties: No Economic Realignment Fueling Their Success. *European Journal of Political Research*, 44, 465–492.

Ivarsflaten, E. (2008) What Unites the Populist Right in Western Europe? Reexamining Grievance Mobilization Models in Seven Successful Cases. *Comparative Political Studies*, 41(1), 3–23.

Iversen, T. and Cusack, T. (2000) The Causes of Welfare State Expansion: Deindustrialization or Globalization? *World Politics*, 52, 313–349.

Iversen, T. and Soskice, D. (2015) Democratic Limits to Redistribution: Inclusionary versus Exclusionary Coalitions in the Knowledge Economy. *World Politics*, 67, 185–225.

Kimmel, E. (2013) *Angry White Men: American Masculinity at the End of an Era*. New York: Public Affairs.

Kitschelt, H. (1994) *The Transformation of European Social Democracy*. Cambridge: Cambridge University Press.

Kitschelt, H. (2004) Diversification and Reconfiguration of Party Systems in Postindustrial Democracies. Working Paper. International Policy Analysis Unit, Friedrich-Ebert-Stiftung.

Kitschelt, H. and Rehm, P. (2014) Occupations as a Site of Preference Formation. *Comparative Political Studies*, 47, 1670–1706.

Kitschelt, H. and Rehm, P. (2022) Polarity Reversal: The Socioeconomic Reconfiguration of Partisan Support in Knowledge Societies, *Politics & Society* (OnlineFirst). https://doi.org/10.1177/00323292221100220.

Kitschelt, H. and Wilkinson, S. (2007) *Patrons, Clients and Policies: Patterns of Democratic Accountability and Political Competition*. New York: Cambridge University Press.

Knutsen, O. (2006) *Class Voting in Western Europe*. Lanham, MD: Lexington Books.

Knutsen, O. (2018) *Social Structure, Value Orientations and Party Choice in Western Europe*. Cham: Palgrave Macmillan.

Kriesi, H. and Schulte-Cloos, J. (2020) Support for Radical Parties in Western Europe: Structural Conflicts and Political Dynamics. *Electoral Studies*, 65(1), 102–138.

Kriesi, H., Grande, E., Lachat, R., et al. (2006) Globalization and the Transformation of the National Political Space: Six European Countries Compared. *European Journal of Political Research*, 45, 921–956.

Kriesi, H., Grande, E., Lachat, R., et al., eds. (2008) *West European Politics in the Age of Globalization*. Cambridge: Cambridge University Press.

Kriesi, H., Kiipmans, R., Dyvendak, J. W., and Giugni, M. G. (1995) *New Social Movements in Western Europe: A Comparative Analysis*. London: UCL Press.

Lachat, M. (2008) The Electoral Consequences of the Integration–Demarcation Cleavage. In H. P. Kriesi, E. Grande, R. Lachat, et al., eds., *West European Politics in the Age of Globalization*. Cambridge: Cambridge University Press, pp. 296–319.

Lancaster, C. M. (2022) Value Shift: Immigration Attitudes and the Sociocultural Divide. *British Journal of Political Science*, 52, 1–20.

Laver, M. (1998) Models of Government Formation. *Annual Review of Political Science*, 1, 1–25.

Lefkofridi, Z. and Michel, E. (2017) The Electoral Politics of Solidarity. In K. Banting and W.Kymlicka, eds., *The Strains of Commitment*. New York: Oxford University Press, pp. 233–276.

Lefkofridi, Z., Wagner, M., and Willmann, J. E. (2014) Left Authoritarians and Policy Representation in Western Europe: Electoral Choice across Ideological Dimensions. *West European Politics*, 37, 65–90.

Liberini, F., Redoanao, M., Russo, A., Cuevas, A., and Cuevas, R. (2020) Politics in the Facebook Era: Evidence from the 2016 US Presidential Elections. Working Paper. University of Warwick.

Lowe, W., Benoit, K., Mikhaylov, S., and Laver, M. (2011) Scaling Policy Preferences from Coded Political Texts. *Legislative Studies Quarterly*, 36, 123–155.

Magistro, B. and Wittstock, N. (2021) Changing Preferences versus Issue Salience: The Political Success of Anti-Immigration Parties in Italy. *South European Society and Politics*, 26(3), 383–411.

Mannheim, K. (1952) The Problem of Generations. In P. Kecskemeti, ed., *Karl Mannheim: Essays*. London: Routledge, pp. 276–322.

Manow, P., Palier, B., and Schwander, H., eds., (2018) *Welfare Democracies and Party Politics*. Oxford: Oxford University Press.

Marks, G., Attewell, D., Rovny, J., and Hooghe, L. (2021) Cleavage Theory. In M. Riddervold, J. Trondal, and A. Newsome, eds., *The Palgrave Handbook of EU Crises*. Cham: Palgrave, pp. 173–193.

Marks, G., Attewell, D., Hooghe, L., Rovny, J., and Steenbergen, M. (2022) The Social Bases of Political Parties: A New Measure and Survey. *British Journal of Political Science*, 53(1), 249–260.

McDonald, M. and Budge, I. (2005) *Elections, Parties and Democracy: Conferring the Median Mandate*. Oxford: Oxford University Press.

Meguid, B. M. (2005) Competition between Unequals: The Role of Mainstream Party Strategy in Niche Party Success. *American Political Science Review*, 99(3), 347–359.

Meyer, T. M. and Wagner, M. (2020) Perceptions of Parties Left–Right Positions: The Impact of Salience Strategies. *Party Politics*, 26(5) 664–674.

Mierke-Zatwarnicki, A. (2022) Outsider Parties and Appeals to Group Representation: A Macro-Historical Approach. Paper presented to a Workshop on Cleavage Formation in the 20th Century, University of Zurich.

Mosimann, N. and Pontusson, J. (2017) Solidaristic Unionism and Support for Redistribution in Contemporary Europe. *World Politics*, 69, 448–492.

Mosimann, N., Rennwald, L., and Zimmermann, A. (2019) The Radical Right, the Labour Movement and the Competition for the Workers' Vote. *Economic and Industrial Democracy*, 40(1), 65–90.

Mudde, C. (2007) *Populist Radical Right Parties in Europe*. Cambridge: Cambridge University Press.

Norris, P. and Inglehart, R. (2019) *Cultural Backlash: Trump, Brexit and Authoritarian Populism*. Cambridge: Cambridge University Press.

OECD. (2017) Migration Data Brief, No. 2 (December). www.oecd.org/migration/mig/migration-data-brief-2.pdf.

Oesch, D. (2006) *Redrawing the Class Map*. Basingstoke: Palgrave Macmillan.

Oesch, D. (2008a) The Changing Shape of Class Voting: An Individual-Level Analysis of Party Support in Britain, Germany and Switzerland. *European Societies*, 10, 329–355.

Oesch, D. (2008b) Explaining Workers' Support for Right-Wing Populist Parties in Western Europe: Evidence from Austria, Belgium, France, Norway and Switzerland. *International Political Science Review*, 29(3), 349–373.

Oesch, D. (2013a) *Occupational Change in Europe*. Oxford: Oxford University Press.

Oesch, D. (2013b) The Class Basis of the Cleavage between the New Left and the Radical Right: An Analysis for Austria, Denmark, Norway and Switzerland. In J. Rydgren, ed., *Class Politics and the Radical Right*. Abingdon: Routledge, pp. 31–51.

Oesch, D. and Rennwald, L. (2018) Electoral Competition in Europe's New Tripolar Political Space: Class Voting for the left, Centre-Right and Radical Right. *European Journal of Political Research*, 44, 465–492.

Otjes, S. and Krouwel, A. (2022) Environmental Policy Preferences and Economic Interests in the Nature/Agriculture and Climate/Energy Dimension in the Netherlands. *Rural Sociology*, 87(3), 901–935.

Palier, B. and Thelen, K. (2010) Institutionalizing Dualism: Complementarities and Change in France and Germany. *Politics & Society*, 38, 119–148.

Peck, J. (2001) *Workfare States*. New York: Guilford Press.

Peugny, C. (2019) The Decline in Middle-Skilled Employment in 12 European Countries: New Evidence for Job Polarisation. *Research and Politics*, 6(1). https://doi.org/10.1177/2053168018823131.

Pierson, P., ed. (2001) *The New Politics of the Welfare State*. New York: Oxford University Press.

Pierson, P. (2003) Big, Slow-Moving . . . and Invisible: Macrosocial Processes in the Study of Comparative Politics. In J. Mahoney and D. Rueschemeyer, eds.,*Comparative Historical Analysis in the Social Sciences*. New York: Cambridge University Press, pp. 177–207.

Poguntke, T. (1987) New Politics and Party Systems: The Emergence of a New Type of Party?*West European Politics*, 10(1), 76–88.

Polk, J. and Rovny J. (2018) Welfare Democracies and Multidimensional Party Competition in Europe. In P. Manow, B. Palier, and H. Schwander, eds., *Welfare Democracies and Party Politics*. Oxford: Oxford University Press, pp. 29–60.

Pontusson, J. (2005) *Inequality and Prosperity: Social Europe vs. Liberal America*. Ithaca, NY: Cornell University Press.

Rehm, P. (2016) *Risk Inequality and Welfare States*. New York: Cambridge University Press.

Rohrschneider, R., Miles, M., and Peffley, M. (2014) The Structure and Sources of Global Environmental Attitudes. In R. Dalton and C. Welzel, eds., *The Civic Culture Transformed*. New York: Cambridge University Press, pp. 193–212.

Rommel, T. and Walter, S (2018) The Electoral Consequences of Offshoring: How the Globalization of Production Shapes Party Preferences. *Comparative Political Studies*, 51, 621–658.

Rovny, J. and Polk, J. (2019a) New Wine in Old Bottles: Explaining the Dimensional Structure of European Party Systems. *Party Politics*, 25(1), 12–24.

Rovny J. and Polk, J. (2019b) Still Blurry?: Economic Salience, Position and Voting for Radical Right Parties in Western Europe. *European Journal of Political Research*, 59(2), 248–268.

Rüdig, W., Bennie, L. G., and Franklin, M. N. (1991) *Green Party Members: A Profile*. Glasgow: Delta.

Rueda, D. (2005) Insider–Outsider Politics in Industrialized Democracies: The Challenge to Social Democratic Parties. *American Political Science Review*, 99, 61–74.

Rydgren, J. (2009) Social Isolation? Social Capital and Radical Right-Wing Voting in Western Europe. *Journal of Civil Society*, 5(2), 129–150.

Rydgren, J. ed. (2013) *Class Politics and the Radical Right*, Abingdon: Routledge.

Samejima F. F. (1969) Estimation of Latent Ability Using a Response Pattern of Graded Scores. *Psychometrika*, 34 (Suppl 1), 1–97.

Schmidt, V. and Thatcher, M. (2014) *Resilient Liberalism in Europe's Political Economy*. Cambridge: Cambridge University Press.

Schwander, H. (2020) Labor Market Insecurity among the Middle Class: A Cross-Pressured Group. *Political Science Research and Methods*, 8, 369–374.

Scott, R. (2022) Does University Make You More Liberal? Estimating the Within-Individual Effects of Higher Education on Political Values. *Electoral Studies*, 77. https://doi.org/10.1016/j.electstud.2022.102471.

Silva, B. C. and Wratil, C. (2023) Do Parties' Representation Failures Affect Populist Attitudes? Evidence from a Multinational Survey Experiment. *Political Science Research and Methods*, 11(2), 347–362.

Soroka, S. and Wlezien, C. (2010) *Degrees of Democracy: Politics, Public Opinion, Policy*. Cambridge: Cambridge University Press.

Spies, D. (2013) Explaining Working-Class Support for Extreme Right Parties: A Party Competition Approach. *Acta Politica*, 48(3), 296–325.

Spruyt, B., Keppens, G., and Van Droogenbroeck, F. (2016) Who Supports Populism and What Attracts People to It? *Political Research Quarterly* 69(2), 335–346.

Talshir, G. (2002) *The Political Ideology of Green Parties*. Basingstoke: Palgrave Macmillan.

Tavits, M. and Potter, J. D. (2015) The Effect of Inequality and Social Identity on Party Strategies. *American Journal of Political Science*, 59(3), 744–758.

Thelen, K. (2014) *Varieties of Liberalization and the New Politics of Social Solidarity*. New York: Cambridge University Press.

Thomson, R., Royed, T., Naurin, E., et al. (2017) The Fulfillment of Parties Election Pledges: A Comparative Study on the Impact of Power Sharing. *American Journal of Political Science*, 61(3), 527–542.

Van der Brug, W. and van Spanje, J. (2009) Immigration, Europe and the New Cultural Dimension. *European Journal of Political Research*, 48, 309–344.

van Haute, E., ed. (2016) *Green Parties in Europe*. London: Routledge.

Volkens, A., Krause, W., Lehmann, P., et al. (2018) *The Manifesto Data Collection*. Berlin: Wissenschaftszentrum Berlin für Sozialforschung.

Wagner, M. and Meyer, T. M. (2017) The Radical Right as Niche Parties? The Ideological Landscape of Party Systems in Western Europe, 1980–2014. *Political Studies*, 65(Suppl 1), 84–107.

Ward, D., Kim, J. H., Graham, M., and Tavits, M. (2015) How Economic Integration Affects Party Issue Emphases. *Comparative Political Studies*, 48(10), 1227–1259.

Weakliem D. L. (2002) The Effects of Education on Political Opinions: An International Study. *International Journal of Public Opinion Research*, 14(2), 141–157.

Wren, A., ed. (2013) *The Political Economy of the Service Transition*. Oxford: Oxford University Press.

Wren, A. and Rehm, P. (2013) Service Expansion, International Exposure and Political Preferences. In A. Wren, ed., *The Political Economy of the Service Transition*. Oxford: Oxford University Press, pp. 248–281.

Acknowledgments

For helpful comments on earlier drafts of this Element, we are grateful to participants in a Workshop on Cleavage Formation in the 21st Century at the University of Zurich, organized by Silja Häusermann and Delia Zollinger, and to participants in the Seminar on Comparative Politics at the London School of Economics and Political Science, organized by Catherine Boone, Steffen Hertog, and Jonathan Hopkin, and for which David Soskice provided crucial support. We thank Waltraud Schelkle, Rosemary C. R. Taylor, and Linus Westheuser for especially detailed comments and Arthur Goldhammer for assistance calculating the viability of coalitions. We are grateful to Gary Marks and Catherine De Vries for encouraging us to submit this manuscript to their Elements in European Politics series and for the comments of two anonymous reviewers. The research for this Element was supported by a faculty research grant from the Weatherhead Center for International Affairs at Harvard University.

Cambridge Elements ≡

European Politics

Catherine De Vries

Bocconi University

Catherine De Vries is a Dean of International Affairs and Professor of Political Science at Bocconi University. Her research revolves around some of the key challenges facing the European continent today, such as Euroscepticism, political fragmentation, migration and corruption. She has published widely in leading political science journals, including the *American Political Science Review* and the *Annual Review of Political Science*. She has published several books, including *Euroscepticism and the Future of European integration* (Oxford University Press), received the European Union Studies Association Best Book in EU Studies Award, and was listed in the *Financial Times* top-5 books to read about Europe's future.

Gary Marks

University of North Carolina at Chapel Hill and European University Institute

Gary Marks is Burton Craige Professor at the University of North Carolina, Chapel Hill, and Professor at the European University Institute, Florence. He has received the Humboldt Forschungspreis and the Daniel Elazar Distinguished Federalism Scholar Award. Marks has been awarded an Advanced European Research Council grant (2010–2015) and is currently senior researcher on a second Advanced European Research Council grant. He has published widely in leading political science journals, including the *American Political Science Review* and the *American Journal of Political Science*. Marks has published a dozen books, including *A Theory of International Organization* and *Community, Scale and Regional Governance*.

Advisory Board

Sara Hobolt, *London School of Economics*
Sven-Oliver Proksch, *University of Cologne*
Jan Rovny, *Sciences Po, Paris*
Stefanie Walter, *University of Zurich*
Rahsaan Maxwell, *University of North Carolina, Chapel Hill*
Kathleen R. McNamara, *Georgetown University*
R. Daniel Kelemen, *Rutgers University*
Carlo Altomonte, *Bocconi University*

About the Series

The Cambridge Elements Series in European Politics will provide a platform for cutting-edge comparative research on Europe at a time of rapid change for the disciplines of political science and international relations. The series is broadly defined, both in terms of subject and academic discipline. The thrust of the series will be thematic rather than ideographic. It will focus on studies that engage key elements of politics — e.g. how institutions work, how parties compete, how citizens participate in politics, how laws get made.

Cambridge Elements ≡

European Politics

Elements in the Series

Political Change and Electoral Coalitions in Western Democracies
Peter A. Hall, Georgina Evans and Sung In Kim

A full series listing is available at: www.cambridge.org/EEP

Printed in the United States
by Baker & Taylor Publisher Services